Our Hearts' Desire

For Families Navigating
the Journey of
Sensory Processing Challenges

Marci Laurel, MA, CCC-SLP
& Carla Cay Williams, OT/L

"I highly recommend this book. The decades of Marci's experience as a mother and speech-language pathologist beautifully weave together with the decades of Carla's experience as an occupational therapist supporting this family and so many others. When I read *Our Hearts' Desire* I was inspired, as I know you will be, by the dedication, commitment, and love of so many who participated along this family's journey. These outstanding international speakers have captured the highlights of their remarkable journey so you can learn from their wisdom, touching stories and practical suggestions."

Mary Sue Williams
Co-author of the Alert Program®

"This book is an incredible gift to parents whose children face sensory processing challenges. It provides personal and professional insight into the difficulties that many parents experience trying to understand their child's confusing and often overwhelming behavior. With humor and love, Marci and Carla provide personal examples and practical strategies to help children, their families, and all of us around them, gain a better and more compassionate understanding of what it is like to live with sensory processing challenges."

Courtney Burnette, Ph.D.
Clinical Psychologist

"Finally, a book that empowers rather than makes me feel like a failure. This is a book that I can pick up for inspiration when "it" all feels like too much and I am drowning alone in all of the work that it takes to help my son overcome his individual roadblocks.

His roadblocks are different than those of his peers — and that is okay. Here is my reminder that I have assembled a team to help him and that he is okay. Here is my reminder of good ways to nurture that team. Here is my reminder that it is okay to need that team."

Erica Bourdon
Mother of a child with ASD

"If you have picked up this book, chances are you have some questions and concerns about a child's development and possibly, challenging behavior. You may be struggling to deal with a "diagnosis" and a variety of opinions regarding what to do about it. You may be hoping for someone who has been there to talk to but may be feeling pretty isolated. Professional opinions may be easier to come by but who among them best understands?

Our Hearts' Desire is a collection of insights into the sometimes funny, sometimes poignant or painful experiences and memories of working to grow as a family and to understand and support children who do not follow typical patterns. It is also a wonderfully practical guide to navigating the journey from infancy and toddlerhood though the maze of school years that can be frustrating, scary and confusing as well as deeply rewarding.

Our Hearts' Desire reflects not only the hopes and wisdom of a family. It reveals the experience, expertise, passion and wisdom of two gifted professionals who have dedicated their life's work to those quirky, different and sometimes hard to love kids. You will find within these pages supportive and helpful companions to offer understanding, work through the hard questions, deal out some tough love and provide practical, reasonable suggestions – all presented with compassion, integrity and respect.

This little book will become your guide as you seek your "heart's desire" of the deep gratification of helping that different kid become all s/he can be!"

Maryann Trott, BCBA
Educator and Mom

"Sensory integration problems, now usually known as Sensory Processing Disorders, can be baffling for parents to identify and understand. Very often parents are told that their child's behavior is due to lack of parenting skills or that their child is misbehaving. Often parents feel something is just not quite right with their child but are not able to initially identify what it is about their child that does not seem to fit. They may be told by other professionals such as doctors that their child is just "being a boy" or that the child will grow out of it. These mixed messages can be challenging for parents to deal with.

In Our Hearts' Desire, Marci Laurel and Carla Cay Williams present a beautifully written guide for parents to help navigate these uncertain waters. Through their own personal experiences as a parent and as occupational and speech therapists, they present both the parental voice and practical professional information. As they take you through a child's development from infancy through adolescence and to young adulthood, they provide guidance on what to look for, how to handle questions from families and other professionals, and most importantly, how to trust yourself as parents who know their child.

Many books available to parents today that are written by parents may not adequately or accurately represent sensory integration theory or activities. With Marci and Carla's years of experience working with children with sensory integration problems, they provide the most accurate information and resources for parents on sensory integration from what to look for, to sample letters for families and doctors, to scripts on what to say when others don't understand your child.

This book is a delight to read and presents information that is useable not only for parents with a child with SPD but also those with children on the autism spectrum. I am delighted to have the opportunity to recommend this book to parents and teachers."

Teresa A. May-Benson, ScD, OTR/L, FAOTA
Executive Director of Research of the Spiral Foundation

Dedication

This book is dedicated with the deepest appreciation to my sons, my patient and most excellent teachers. I could never express the depth of the love and admiration I feel for you both – you guys are a light beyond my wildest dreams.

And in loving memory of Dr. Jane Koomar, brilliant occupational therapist whose intellect was matched only by her loving heart. Jane, your wisdom, encouragement, free sharing of knowledge and direct contributions mean more than can possibly be imagined. You are dearly missed, still we feel you here in everything we do, calling upon us to be the best of ourselves. This labor of love will always be a part yours in our hearts.

Acknowledgements

First, both Carla and I acknowledge Patti Oetter with profound appreciation and love. She introduced me to what I never knew yet always knew, took me on so many exhilarating adventures and helped me to find my voice, my hands and my heart. We are also both forever indebted to Sue Windeck for all that she taught us about sensory integration. I continue to be influenced daily by the extraordinary and intimate experience of co-treatment that she shared with me so freely. Our lifelong appreciation to all of the therapists who worked at Albuquerque Therapy Services in the late 1980s - our time together remains a professional high-light of our lives.

I am forever grateful to the family and friends who have cared for my children and me and walked with us along the way – Mary Sue Williams and Sherry Shellenberger were literally there from the beginning, loved the boys and helped me know my own heart; Susan Smith has been a member of our family in every sense of the word, providing never ending support and love in all aspects of our lives including (if not most importantly) homework and science fair; Bob, Debra and Rachel Sugar have provided a tremendous and precious New Mexico extended family, joyful connection and a yearly soccer match where everyone belongs; Mary Jo Daniel gave early every week support rain or shine and has continued to be there for us in the many years since Park of the Bridges; my dear birthday buddies and remarkable women: Mo Taylor, Lori Lange, Wendy Kalberg and Kim Willard have shown me the safest harbor of friendship and shared motherhood; Maryann Trott has been mentor, friend and spiritual beacon; Carol Price felt deeply with me as we tried our very best to smooth the bumps in the roads of our children; Suzanne Carlson shared her unique capacity to listen, see, remember and love with passion and without judgment; Val Ford has been a steady touch stone helping me learn and then learn again my own truth; Kathryn Faturos has been my excellent workout partner bringing energy and stress management and always cheerleading for the guys; the Hausers have been our sweet, loving and always waiting for us family in Florida. Thanks so much to Mo for a mother's lifetime of friendship and freely shared consultation and to Wendy for far too much to name. I can't imagine motherhood without the every single day support and endless processing shared with Debra whose unconditional love for all of us is a gift beyond measure. To my sister Bucky I give thanks for always seeing the best in my boys and the countless hours of supportive sharing and ranting from so many miles away. To my brother Steve my deep appreciation for loving and understanding the guys uniquely, and also and especially for believing in me first. Enormous and forever love and gratitude to "Papa and Ling Ling" who profoundly supported our parenting, loved and cherished the boys in a way no one else could have and were the best grandparents imaginable – we feel you still, "nearer than near."

So many educators have significantly shaped the trajectory of the boys' lives. I am indebted to Albuquerque Preschool Cooperative, Zia Elementary School, Bellehaven Elementary School, 21st Century Public Academy and Albuquerque High School. There are no words to thank Wendy Wyman, Helene Abrams, Carol Jenkins, Linda Mahan, Anne Bullock, Kay Maize, Carrie McGill, Peggy Brown, Dennis Higgins, Jennifer Jewel, Maryann Stone, Donna Eldridge, Peter Doane, Connie Hudgeons and the many, many other teachers whose work matters more than they can probably imagine.

Thanks to so many who took the time to edit our manuscript with tender loving care: Jane Bluestein, Erica Bourdon, Suzanne Carlson, Mary Jo Daniel, Val Ford, Robyn Elison, Phoebe Grindal, Beth Hauser, Wendy Kalberg, Lauriann King, Joni Kleinman, Patricia Lemer, Mary Mccarthy, Patti Oetter, Craig Pierce, Eileen Richter, Susan Smith, Debra Sugar, Maryann Trott, Martha Wenderoth, Jack Wilder, Kim Willard, Mary Sue Williams and Jean Anne Zollars. Much love and appreciation to Wendy Wyman, PJ and Bob's first teacher, for helping us understand the needs of the smallest children, Alice Luna for insight about the thinking of a pediatrician and Debra and Suzanne for insight and humor about parenting from day to day. Great appreciation to Erica and Lauriann for their parent perspectives, honest feedback and steadfast belief in this work. Huge thanks to Elise Trott for her amazing ability to translate our thoughts and feelings into the beautiful graphic for the cover, to the Youngs for sharing their family to make the cover possible, and to Amy Schulz for taking the cover all the way and applying her considerable talents to finishing the whole project. Much appreciation to Eileen for giving me a chance way back when, ongoing professional support and generous attention to detail feedback. Mary Sue slogged through from beginning to end, listening, brainstorming, encouraging and finally helping with the eleventh hour editing, continually and gently reminding me that life, both with my boys and with this writing, would unfold exactly as it should.

Molly McEwen became a part of this project toward the finish and not a moment too soon! So many thanks for believing in our work with characteristic love and direct communication, providing invaluable feedback given with exquisite respect and remarkable clarity. Jane Bluestein emerged as our champion over the final year, quietly yet persistently encouraging forward motion and extending to me her extraordinary love. Much appreciation to Courtney Burnette for a final read-though, but more importantly for creating together an exceptional space of connection, including heartfelt support for my current stage of parenting, helping me to choose love over fear each day. To Teresa May-Benson, I could never express what it means to have you step in for Jane in these last months, providing connection to the beautiful Dr. Koomar while bringing your own special and invaluable contribution.

All of our love to the therapists at KidPower, past and present, who carry this work forward with remarkable belief and focus. Of course and always, we owe an immeasurable debt to all of the children and their families who have been our teachers for the past 30 years. Every single one of you has helped unlock a small piece of the mystery and brought a great deal of delight.

What to say about my wildly talented colleague, dear friend, co-teacher, travel partner, forever therapist to my children and at last co-author Carla – I could never adequately express the extraordinary gift you are in my life and in the lives of so many. Finally Jack. Whatever they said about us, only we could have brought our two beautiful boys into this world! You are an amazing father and the direct link to so much that you admire in the guys – I hope you can come to truly believe that what you see when you look at them is a clear reflection of everything that you are and were given to be.

— Marci Laurel

Contents

Foreword

By Lauriann King

If you are a parent of a child with sensory integration dysfunction, or you work with children with Sensory Processing Disorder, you have just found the ultimate guide for your unique journey. This is the basic survival guide that every parent and professional seeks to address the complicated issues related to sensory integration. It offers practical strategies that can help us to help those we love to enjoy life to its fullest.

My son has a diagnosis of autism and sensory integration issues have been a major part of his development. As a parent, I perceived sensory integration issues as mysterious and complicated, only to be understood by few professionals. At the same time, I knew that it was part of my son and explained why he would cover his ears with a look of pain when I turned on the vacuum cleaner. I have had so many experiences with my child where I was confused about his reaction and later learned that it was related to sensory integration issues. Addressing these issues has played an incredible role in his growth and successes. In my role as a Family Specialist, I interact with parents who also struggle with these challenges on a daily basis in my work. Like you and me, they are also on this path and seeking a resource that relates practical ways to help our children.

This book is different from other resources you may have read. Though it offers much practical information that you will need, it goes beyond and walks readers down the unique path from the parent's perspective, addressing common life situations such as dealing with family members and friends and trusting your own feelings. It speaks to the parent's soul with encouragement, empowerment and understanding. The reader learns the insightful wisdom from a parent who has already walked down the path and helps us to embrace the uniqueness of our own journey.

It is clearly evident, when reading this book, that the authors are experts in the field of sensory integration, in addition to their love for children and families. I know this on a personal level because they have both worked as professionals with my son. Over the past nine years, my son has received both individual occupational therapy and group therapy from Carla Cay Williams at KidPower Therapy Associates. The area of sensory integration had to be addressed in order for him to learn a variety of other skills such as social skills and language. I have seen Carla integrate many of the strategies described in this book into the therapy setting, and learned from her how to use the strategies in daily life.

I have told Carla many times throughout the years that she is more fearless than a skydiver. In my family's history we have missed many special events for fear of how the noise and crowdedness would affect my son, including birthday parties. While everyone is singing "happy birthday", my son would be screaming and have his fingers in his ears. Carla has worked with us as a family unit to find out what is getting in the way of our life as a family, and fearlessly taken it on. Her knowledge in the area of sensory integration and occupational therapy makes her a remarkable expert in the field, and her passion to help children and families makes her a champion. By the way, Carla attended several birthday parties with us this summer. My son actually sang the happy birthday song with a smile on his face.

Marci Laurel has also worked with my son as a speech therapist. She has consulted with my son's teachers and school staff over the past four years, integrating many of the supports within this book into the classroom setting. The school professionals have used these tools to help my son be included in a regular education classroom with his peers. As you will understand after reading this book, Marci works with a lot of heart and passion for the children she serves.

In third grade, I visited school and realized that my son spent most of recess pacing the perimeter of the playground, with his fingers in his ears. The concern was not necessarily academic, but it impacted the way he was perceived by his peers and his quality of life. Marci saw the importance of this task and worked with the school team on strategies so he could be more successful. Marci has the knowledge to help in these critical areas, and the passion to help children live life fully. Her knowledge in the areas of speech pathology and sensory integration makes her an extraordinary professional. Add her personal experience as a parent and she is on a different playing field from other professionals. I am confident that after reading this book, you will join me in being inspired by her incredible spirit.

If you are on a similar path to mine, I'm so happy for you that you found this book! Get ready to be empowered with information that can help you on a daily basis. If you are seeking practical information in the area of sensory integration that you can easily apply to your life, this book will offer an incredible resource. If you are looking for encouragement and hope for your own personal tomorrow, open these pages and enjoy...

Introduction

As a young speech-language pathologist working in a clinic specializing in treating children with Sensory Processing Disorders, I was excited—exhilarated even—learning about this incredible body of information, living life (professionally speaking) on the cutting edge. But, when early in my marriage, my occupational therapist mentors suggested that when my husband Jack and I had a child we should bring the baby in for sensory integration treatment immediately, I was somewhat offended. Okay, so Jack and I had met in a 6:00AM aerobics class that we attended faithfully. Okay, so maybe it wasn't the best idea for two people who needed this type of intense activity first thing in the morning to be mixing their genetic pools. And true, Jack and I did seem to have some problems similar to the kids that came to the clinic every day. But we were in love. What could happen?

When our son PJ was born we were as excited as any new parents. He was healthy and beautiful and we were so very lucky. We were overwhelmed, of course, and read all the suggested books cover to cover. We watched our little baby in awe and in wonder. But when PJ struggled to learn to nurse during the first six weeks of his life, in spite of the best advice I could attain, I became anxious and frustrated, and a little nagging voice of worry began to settle itself in my heart.

We talked to friends and family about our struggles with sleep deprivation. Everyone had a story, and was more than happy to tell it, about the early months and lack of sleep. We were assured that our baby would "settle" sometime soon. But we did not hear much about babies who woke every ten minutes for hour after hour each night, only to fall back to sleep and wake up again. And luckily, we did not know at that time that our son would not sleep through the night until he was more than four years old. Later, when PJ seemed to have difficulty getting motivated to move, when lack of movement was followed by periods of irritability, when motor skills did not develop at the expected rate and when our little boy grew into a toddler who seemed to spend a lot of time in a world that was hard for others to share, that worry took up permanent residence in my heart.

We were very fortunate to have available to us some of the country's leading experts in sensory integration. We used many techniques to support PJ's development and he began to receive direct occupational therapy services as a very young child. All of the help, and the amazing therapists who supported us through those early times, had an incredible impact on our son and on our lives. Still, in many ways, the journey was just beginning. PJ has since been our teacher through all the stages of his life, helping us understand more about sensory integration, yes, but also about true love and acceptance, about persistence and courage, about working as part of a team in ways that I had never thought possible. Throughout this journey my colleague and dear friend,

Carla Cay Williams, has been an unfailing, brilliant and sustaining member of our team and an inextricable part of our family's story.

When PJ was about 22 months old, we had a big surprise. Jack and I found out that my sudden waves of exhaustion and sickness were not, as I secretly feared, the result of some life threatening illness. Instead, while we were trying so hard to understand PJ and to settle into our life as a family, I had become pregnant and for almost three months neglected to notice! All through the remainder of my pregnancy Jack, forgoing appeals for world peace and brotherly love, prayed for only one thing— "Let the new baby be a sleeper." Well, he got his wish. Our new baby boy, Bob, was a wonderful sleeper. He also nursed easily and well, was easy going and content, made transitions like a champ and worshipped his big brother. I still remember going to a parent conference when Bob was attending a preschool program for two-year-olds and the teacher saying she simply could not think of a single goal to work on with Bob. We had our "regular" boy.

But in retrospect, Jack could have been more specific in his nightly petition. Regrettably, he forgot to say—"Let the new baby have eyes that work well together. Let him develop integrated reflexes, core stability and bilateral integration. And please, let the new baby be able to succeed in school." So Bob was our second little professor, teaching us about life in school for children with learning disabilities, helping us to understand more fully the role of the eyes and the body in development and, especially, showing us up close and very personally the frustration and anger as well as the bravery and fortitude that can become a part of the effort *to keep on trying when the only daily work available for a little person is the very thing that comes the hardest.*

For nearly three decades, I have been passionately involved in the study of Sensory Processing Disorder as a speech-language pathologist, as a teacher and most profoundly as the mother of my own two children. It is my wish to share a piece of what I have learned, both practically and spiritually, about the things that I have discovered. Most importantly, I ache for a way to express the bottomless feelings that I have experienced, and that other parents have shared with me, about our hearts' deepest desire—to see all of our children as whole and complete and on the path to having the happiest life possible. To see all of our children truly belong.

1

An Overview of Sensory Integration

From 2000 until 2005, Carla and I had the opportunity to teach a two day course throughout the United States, in collaboration with Professional Education Programs, about sensory integration related to learning and development. At this point, we had long been colleagues as well as a team working on behalf of my own two children, and we had the pleasure of integrating all that we had learned and continued to learn from both a professional and family perspectives. We met amazing parents, educators and therapists through our travels, and received warm feedback indicating that our way of conceptualizing this complex topic was meaningful and useful to their daily practice. We were often asked when we planned to put our work in writing, and so many years later this is our answer to that encouraging request. While there is much excellent written work on the topic of sensory integration, we hope this summary, along with information provided throughout the book, helps to clarify, illuminate and make the information easy to understand in the context of your daily life with your child.

The Senses

Our lives are full of constant, ever changing and at times overwhelming sensory experiences. Dr. A. Jean Ayres, a brilliant occupational therapist and researcher, described sensory integration as our ability to organize these experiences for use in making sense of this complicated sensory world (Ayres, 1979, p. 5). Through her clinical observations and her in-depth understanding of neuroscience, she was one of the first practitioners to recognize the importance of the body's ability to process information through all of the senses beginning in early development. We receive information from our senses to learn about our body and about how to understand what is happening beyond our body and in the world around us. As we are developing this basic foundation, the stage is being set for us to learn higher level skills such as using our eyes and hands together, focusing and attending, listening and talking, and organizing and managing ourselves in a variety of environments. The theory of sensory integration, the assessments, the intervention techniques and the therapy equipment used today are all an outgrowth of Dr. Ayres' groundbreaking work.

Most of us were taught early on that we have five senses: seeing, hearing, touch, taste and smell. Of these five basic senses, the ability of our body to understand and process information received from touch input is one of the most important. Touch, or tactile input, involves more than just what touches our skin.

Touch information is perceived on every part of our body. We can feel when the hair on our head, arms or legs is touched. This is often called light touch, and for some of us this input can even be sensed when we are simply exposed to air, wind, or changes in temperature on our skin. Our skin also receives information from deep pressure touch and this, in combination with input from our muscles and joints, is the kind of input that helps us develop body awareness. This awareness provides us with an understanding of our own body parts, allows us to gain fine motor control of objects in our mouths and hands, and also helps us with the placement of our feet for walking and running. Even our internal organs process information from touch, so we know when we are full while eating or when we need to go to the bathroom. When our sense of touch is working efficiently, common experiences such as wearing clothes, brushing against others in a crowd, taking a shower or getting a hug, feel comfortable and safe. Because our mouths also have very sensitive touch receptors, when the touch system is functioning well, we are more likely to be able to eat a variety of foods with different tastes, textures and temperatures, and learn to articulate clearly when we talk.

The theory of sensory integration includes two other senses that are very important to our overall state of wellbeing and ability to navigate through life. One that we do not usually learn about in school is our sense of balance, and also includes our sense of movement through space. This is called the vestibular sense, because this system receives and processes information in a "vestibule" or chamber in our inner ear. This vestibular system is made up of canals and gravity receptors, and every time our head moves in any way and into any position the movement sends messages through nerve fibers to tell the brain exactly where the body is in space, e.g., right side up, upside down, moving fast or slow and in what direction. The most noticeable skills this movement system helps us develop are balance and the coordination of both sides of our bodies to perform activities such as jumping, bike riding and catching balls. This system also sends messages to the eyes to help us coordinate our visual system with our movements so that the eyes, the hands and the body all work together. Examples of this eye-hand integration are the ability to maneuver around objects, to play games with a ball, to cut on a line, or to easily form letters and organize information on a paper when writing or drawing. Because the vestibular system is located in the inner ear, both the auditory and vestibular systems are part of one whole system. The vestibular system responds to movement, while the auditory system responds to sounds. Therefore, there are many influences of the vestibular portion on the auditory portion that directly affect our auditory processing (the ability to listen and understand) and our language development. When the visual and auditory systems are functioning well together with the vestibular system, we are better able to attend with our eyes and ears, understand what we see and hear and express ourselves easily in conversation or in writing.

Yet another lesser known sense is called proprioception. Proprioceptive input comes from information received through our muscles and joints. This system works with our touch system to provide us with a body scheme from which to gain an understanding of where our body boundaries end and the rest of the world begins. The proprioceptive system also works together with our vestibular system to help us balance and develop muscle tone for postural skills like sitting still and upright while eating at the dinner table or while handwriting. When this proprioceptive system is receiving sufficient input, we experience a feeling of control because our brain knows exactly where each part of our body is and how it is moving. Once we have practiced new skills, our proprioceptive system, together with our tactile system, helps us to automatically perform every day activities such as dressing ourselves, tying our shoes, sequencing our morning routine, driving a car or playing sports, and ultimately allows for the ability to easily organize our lives as we move through each day. The proprioceptive system is also very important to our emotional wellbeing. It helps us to feel grounded and is very useful for helping us to regain control after an upset. Many adults develop physical routines for themselves, such as weight training, power walking, running, cycling, or swimming. While commonly considered simply exercise, these types of activities actually provide strong proprioceptive and vestibular input. In fact, many of these same adults frequently speak of experiencing an improved emotional state after intense physical exercise, sometimes referred to as a "runner's high."

What Happens When There Are Sensory Challenges?

When a child demonstrates difficulties processing information through these foundational sensory systems, that child's actions are often interpreted as "behavior problems." For example, some children do not process sensory information well from the tactile and/or vestibular systems. They may be whiny or cling to adults, appear to be bossy or highly controlling, or seem more or less physically active than their peers. These same children may be over-reactive to seemingly minor events or harmless situations, refuse to participate in group activities, or have "melt downs" in places that are very stimulating such as restaurants or large stores. Other children who might not accurately perceive information from their touch system may be described as "consistently inconsistent." These children may avoid different textures with their hands or on their skin and at the same time be constantly touching objects or other people. Similarly they might be called "picky eaters" yet elicit adult concerns because they "put everything in their mouths." Another example would be children who do not accurately perceive information through their vestibular and proprioceptive systems. These children may take excessive risks and demonstrate impulsivity, or may refuse to take risks all together. Some of these children may seem uncaring or unaware of their environment or other people, or have difficulty developing social skills. When maneuvering through crowded environments they are often described as "bulls in the china shop." They may require much more help in performing basic daily activities such as dressing, buttoning, zipping or getting their shoes on the correct feet and tying them. When children with Sensory Processing Disorders (SPD) get to school, difficulty processing combinations of sensory input could lead to concerns about their ability to use their eyes for focused attention for reading or copying from the board, or to use their ears for learning new information and following directions. They may have difficulty organizing their space and materials or developing and maintaining friendships.

Diagnosis and treatment of sensory processing disorder is most commonly implemented by an occupational therapist trained in understanding and evaluating the sensory systems in order to address the specific sensory, motor and developmental needs of each child. Other professionals such as speech-language pathologists or physical therapists might also have this training and can help design individualized programs. When looking for help for children with sensory processing challenges, it is important to seek out professionals who have this specialized training and experience. As a parent, the more you learn about Sensory Processing Disorder and sensory integration theory, assessment and intervention and how it relates to your child, the better prepared you will be to find therapists that can answer your specific questions and work closely with you to design appropriate interventions for your child and family. Resources about sensory processing and sensory integration are plentiful, and some of our favorites are cited at the end of each chapter.

The causes of Sensory Processing Disorder are unknown. Many families report having more than one family member with similar issues. As the number of people with sensory processing challenges in a family increases, so does the complexity of the needs of the family. In some cases, when parents remember similar challenges from their own childhoods, it might allow them to empathize with the day to day struggles of their child in a way no one else can. On the other hand, if a parent's sensory needs do not match the child's sensory needs, it might cause additional challenges and stress on family relationships. We hope that this book will offer insight into Sensory Processing Disorder and the substantial challenges that can arise for some growing children and their families. It is our intention to provide practical information in a developmental framework as well as to share a parent perspective about day to day family life. We wish to be a source of support for the many grown-ups, both parent and professional, who work each day to ensure the best possible quality of life for every child they know.

A glossary of other terms related to sensory integration is provided in *Appendix II*.

2

Infancy:
I Think Something Might Be Wrong!

When we signed on to become parents, what many of us did not realize is that there is a well-organized competition, a Parent-Infant Olympics of sorts, that we all become a part of upon the birth of our child. And in this competition, new families are awarded points for having a "good baby"; that is, one who does not cry much, smiles a lot and is generally easy to get along with. Additional points can be earned by easy feeding, admirable digestion, teething without symptoms and limited illness in the first year of life. Of course, gold medals are only considered for those families who have babies who can sleep through the night!

I found out pretty early on that those of us who are not viable contenders in this "Baby Olympics" develop some pretty strange coping strategies in that first year. In our deepest psyche we envy the baby "stars" and, yes, even sometimes resent our own offspring for failing to reflect on us a positive light. We may also begin to *begrudge the winning families, judging them in whatever ways we can think of, telling ourselves that **our** sons and daughters are actually smarter, more interesting, better looking. And while we tell ourselves that we do not care about this dreadful competition, we hurt inside because the implication all around us is that we are doing something wrong and that other more "successful" parents know something that we do not know. And though we suspect that this might be true, we cannot figure out a way to make things different.*

If you are still in the infancy stage of parenting, this would be a good time to get a handle on the tendency to compare your little one to the children of other people. All babies are different, operating on their own time schedule, marching to the beat of their own internal drummer. And, some babies come into the world with bigger challenges inside of them. In this day and age of rushing and hurrying, it often feels as though there is increased pressure to have child development follow a specific time schedule. The fear that your baby is not conforming to the correct agenda only compounds the added stressors of your own sleep deprivation or dealing with a fussy baby.

I remember being worried too much of the time, about feeding, about sleep, about developmental milestones. It was almost as if worry attracted worry, like a magnet in my heart, making me question too much and blinding me even, at times, to the sweet miracle unfolding in my family.

Try, every day, to let the extraordinary love that you feel for your unique little person be bigger than your fear.

Things You Might Notice

There are some behaviors that might cause a new parent to wonder whether there is reason for worry. Remember that babies, like big people, are unique individuals. They have different temperaments, personalities and preferences. It is important to notice how you feel (as opposed to what your relatives and friends think!) Are you noticing some of the following and feeling concerned?

1. Issues with sleep: You may notice that your baby –
   - Sleeps too much
   - Sleeps too little
   - Seems to have difficulty transitioning from being asleep to being awake
   - Seems restless
   - Has unusual sleep patterns
   - Can only sleep close to another person
   - Can only sleep when held upright
   - Can only fall asleep in the car
   - Can only fall asleep with big movement like walking or bouncing

2. Issues with eating: Your baby might struggle with—
   - Latching on for breast feeding
   - Not eating enough
   - Eating too often
   - Ongoing difficulties transitioning between breast, bottle, and/or pacifier
   - Falling asleep while feeding

- Reflux/Digestion problems (gas, constipation, unusual stools)
- Sucking too hard on the nipple making feeding a challenge
- Difficulty when beginning solid foods

3. Issues with comfort: Your baby seems to—
   - Cry too much, cannot be comforted
   - Cry too little, nothing bothers him/her
   - Be difficult to soothe – standard soothing strategies do not work consistently or only one strategy will work
   - Cry a lot but not in a way that you can understand what it "means"
   - Arch his/her body
   - Dislike being held
   - Stay the same, more like a newborn — he/she does not seem to settle or become more predictable over the first year
   - Prefer to always be in motion
   - Prefer to not be moved much at all
   - Only want to be held upright
   - Be "quiet"; that is, the baby does not babble or make many sounds

Supportive Environments for Infants

The beginning of a human life is a time of extraordinary change and adaptation. The infant emerges from a sensory environment characterized by profound protection and safety - the prenatal world is dark, quiet, rhythmic, warm and provides continual opportunities for deep pressure touch (e.g., as the baby gets bigger in the confined space or pushes with arms and legs against the mother's womb) and various types of movement (babies experience all types of movement before they are born including bouncing, changing position and turning upside down). Not surprisingly, the environment we try to create for the newborn mirrors this special world.

When babies are first born, adults tend to speak to them in quiet voices, wrap them up tightly in blankets and move them in gentle, rhythmical ways. Usually one of the first things a parent will do is put something in the baby's mouth (breast, bottle or pacifier) and, with the exception of that flash camera that is too hard to resist, leave lighting low and soft. These things we naturally know to do, and what follows is a time of parents learning to read the cues of their infants, learning the specifics of what makes their individual baby tick. Even in the first month of life, babies will begin to show a preference for certain types of sensory input. They might prefer looking to listening (e.g., looking at a moving ceiling fan vs. listening to music) or they might be calmed best by sucking or by being moved or by being touched and held frequently. And in the first months of life, they become amazing partners in communication, developing signals using only their eyes and head position to tell us when they want to interact or when they are ready to take a break from being with us. They lead the infant-adult "conversation," taking turns making sounds and moving their bodies in an intricate dance of love and connection. The biggest job for grown-ups is to learn to read the baby's signals and to follow his/her lead. This helps to establish routines that meet the new baby's needs as parent and child guide each other through the first year of life.

Indeed this is a special time of life, but for some babies an inability to organize the brand new barrage of sensory input makes family life challenging from the start. When an infant is unable to achieve a sense of calm and safety in our sensory world, it can be very difficult for the parents to know how to help. New parents are reliant on the cues received from the baby, but infants with sensory processing problems cannot by definition provide these cues, because they are in a constant state of distress (screaming and crying for much of their waking time) or, conversely, are "shut down" to sensory input (sleeping much of the time or seemingly not interested in social interaction). In general, the best sensory strategies for newborns tend to be rhythmic movement (e.g., bouncing, rocking, swaying and vibration), deep pressure touch (e.g., being swaddled or held in a sling), and/or oral-motor stimulation (e.g., breast, bottle, finger or pacifier). Of course, the specific inputs and combinations of input that work for each baby are individual and can change over time, making your daily job as chief "investigator" both a challenge and a reward.

Using Sensory Strategies At Home

Parents of newborns often rely on rocking the baby in a rocking chair, though some newborns seem to prefer front to back movements, so a "Canadian Glider" may be preferable. An additional way of providing movement to infants that some parents have had success with is sitting on an exercise ball holding the baby in their arms while bouncing up and down. For all types of movement input, the adults can experiment with increasing or decreasing the intensity of the movement or changing the rhythm of the movement to see what is most calming to their brand new child.

Many parents report that small children are best calmed by car rides, but this might not be a popular choice when a strategy is needed in the middle of the night! Using an infant seat that can vibrate or placing a supervised infant in a baby seat on top of a running dryer on a padded safe surface can provide the same calming sensory input that the baby enjoys when being driven around town. An added bonus might be catching up on laundry in the dark hours of the night!

Often infants are calmed by deep pressure touch. In many cultures newborns are "worn" in a sling or "snuggly" (e.g., Baby Bjorn or Snuggler) and it is common for parents to swaddle a baby in light blankets. Some parents also learn infant massage techniques. Small babies might respond well to changes in what they hear and see. It can be helpful to try different types of music, singing and various voice pitches. Some babies seem to be calmed by white noise such as listening to the static between local radio stations, having a fan, humidifier or fish tank in the room, or using a commercially sold sleep (white noise) machine. It is generally helpful to keep babies out of fluo-rescent lights and it can be useful to notice a fussy baby's reaction to dark vs. light rooms or changing light stimulation (e.g., moving while facing a window or looking at sparkling lights).

For any baby, sensory strategies that work one day might not work the next. Soothing an infant at this stage may involve flexible experimenting with a variety of approaches. It is always helpful to think back to the sensory environment of the womb space. As new parents who might be dealing with a baby that is struggling to make the transition to our busy and often overwhelming sensory world, think about all the ways that you can recreate those pleasant pre-birth accommodations in your newborn's brand new home. More specific strategies to consider are provided in *Appendix V.*

Childcare

All that you are learning about your unique newborn can guide you in a childcare situation. When infants are spending part of their lives being cared for outside of their home, it is critically important that parents find childcare where they can establish a strong relationship with the childcare providers. Quality childcare for infants will provide a small adult to baby ratio (perhaps 1:3) where the adults are able to respect the individual routines of each baby. This means that the childcare providers will gather detailed information from the parents about eating and sleeping routines at home, as well as the baby's cues and mood changes in the course of a typical day and the comfort strategies that the parents have found successful with their infant. Very early in life, when babies are just beginning to adapt to life in our sensory world, they will not be able to adapt to group routines or expectations. This is especially true in the life of an infant who is having difficulty processing information from his/her senses. This baby will need his/her or her own individual strategies. Specific strategies that parents have already discovered to be calming for their infant should be used in the childcare setting.

The childcare environment for infants should be quiet and calm with enough space to introduce toys or activities a little at a time. It is also important that there be a space in the childcare setting where parents can come and be with their child whenever they are able. For example, nursing mothers need a place to come and nurse their babies, just as other mothers and fathers might be able to visit for feeding or cuddling time. It is also critical to realize that your baby will need to attach to his/her childcare provider. Even though it can be hard to watch your new little baby "falling in love" with a person outside of the family, that developing relationship is a good sign. It indicates that your baby can provide the necessary cues to create the new relationships that will allow him/her to feel comfortable and safe when away from you and your home. Some babies who have had a difficult time getting organized around sleep and wake cycles, eating and/or deriving comfort from adults in their families will need extra time to form these new relationships and, in general, to adjust to childcare outside of their home. If possible, it is important to plan additional time when making the daily transitions to and from childcare, and to make time to communicate with the childcare staff as you work hard to maintain especially close relationships with them. These relationships may take more time and attention when your baby requires additional support.

Trusting Your Feelings

It may be very difficult to trust your feelings at this early stage of parenting because you are so new to the job and because the baby is so small and needs so much. With every concern, you have the feeling that you are making a mountain out of a molehill or conversely, that you are in denial about the enormity of the problem. It is so very important at this stage to keep asking yourself if you think something is wrong in the life of your baby because you feel it inside or because it is what someone else is telling you. It is also important to notice as you approach the end of your child's first year if you feel that the baby is controlling your entire life—almost as if infancy is never ending and there is no sense of the baby settling into some manageable patterns and routines.

At times it was difficult when well-meaning friends suggested, sometimes subtly and other times blatantly, that the struggles we were experiencing were either not really struggles at all or of our own making. While we were certainly new parents with much to learn, our overwhelming sense was that something was different with the development of our baby, and that we therefore needed to deal with our challenges in different ways. When I look back, I might wish I had been more relaxed or wiser or at greater peace, but I do not wish for a single minute that I had tried any less hard to understand and respond to the needs of my special little boy.

Dealing With Family Members and Friends

Dealing with the judgments and expectations of other people can be one of the most challenging aspects of parenting a young child, and this is especially true if your baby is having some difficulties. Some people will tell you that your baby should be on a schedule, and they will have trouble understanding why nothing seems consistent about you or your baby. On the other hand, you might be told that you should not be so rigid about adhering to a schedule, making it hard for you to explain that your little baby seems to be comforted only by routine. Some adults really value a baby's ability to be flexible, going along easily with the adults' normal routines and activities. If this outlook worked for them in the life of their baby, then it might be especially hard for them to understand that your baby was not born to go with the flow! Finally, everyone likes a cheerful baby—one that smiles a lot and makes adorable noises. So if you have a baby who cannot come through with a lot of good-natured behavior, you might feel an overwhelming sense of letting other people down. Beginning to understand some things about the sensory world of your infant might help you to feel more confident in dealing with other people.

More than anything, your new child needs to be able to count on you to try to meet his/her basic needs so that a sense of trust in the world can begin to develop. If you have a compli-cated baby, this job will naturally be more complex. Learning to relate to your family and friends in a way that solicits trust and support will be an important part of your own develop-ment. This might involve gently sharing the information you are discovering about sensory processing with important people in your life, or asking for help in understanding all that you are finding out. On the other hand, you might have to accept that some relationships will not work well at this time in your life. For some, the higher intensity of your child's needs and the magnitude of your own feelings about parenting can create frustration and disappointment that does not allow for a mutually satisfying interaction or friendship.

Considering Professional Help

Sometime during this first year of life, some parents decide to seek professional help from an occupational therapist or other therapists trained in sensory integration assessment and treatment. Signs that it might be time to get outside help could include:

- Developmental milestones such as rolling or sitting are not happening when you think they should or these movements do not look the same or have the same quality as they do for other infants
- Crawling period was brief, began too early or occurred later than expected
- Life feels unmanageable on an ongoing basis and you see no sign of moving toward your days becoming routine or predictable
- Nothing seems to help the baby stop crying and/or there are no specific strategies that work to calm the baby consistently
- The baby will sleep only when being held upright or kept continually moving
- The baby sleeps almost all the time
- The baby does not seem to be motivated to move around as he/she gets older

As you are learning more about sensory integration, it also might be helpful to consider whether either parent or other relatives in the immediate family have experienced similar sensory difficulties throughout their lives. Because these kinds of problems tend to run in families, knowing that there is a family history of sensory problems might help you to decide to seek professional support at this stage of your new baby's life. It can be useful to note that adults who experienced sensory processing difficulties in their own childhood might remember "toughing it out" themselves and therefore be reluctant to pursue professional help. On the other hand, there is a much greater understanding of these challenges today and many parents are hopeful that their young child will be able to benefit from new information through assessment and intervention so that their child can have an easier path.

Dealing with Doctors

Often, when parents are concerned about their baby's life, the first place they seek help is from the pediatrician. These awesome baby doctors offer a wealth of experience for new families and are a wonderful resource. It is important to understand, however, that many pediatricians do not receive training about Sensory Processing Disorder or the warning signs of these difficulties. In addition, some medical practitioners have philosophies that differ from, or are opposed to, the theory and practice of sensory integration based therapies. Sometimes parents are given advice at their doctor visit that creates frustration. For example, the doctor may want to wait awhile to give the baby a chance to settle while continuing to monitor the baby's development instead of immediately making referrals to early intervention or for private or hospital based assessment and/or therapies. This can be difficult for the parents when they have a strong sense that something is really wrong. In addition, it is not unusual for the parents to be told that problems in the family's life are the result of poor parenting, such as a lack of structure or boundaries. The important thing is to find a medical practitioner that you are comfortable with, and for you to feel confident about sharing with him/her what you are learning about your baby and sensory processing. Ultimately, you are the only one who can decide what professional relationships feel right for you and your new baby. Over time, if you feel that your concerns do not make sense to the doctor or you have an ongoing difference of opinion about "waiting and watching" vs. seeking intervention, you might want to look for a new pediatrician who is a better match for your family's unique needs. Some parents seek the perspective of a pediatric neurologist or a developmental pediatrician who specializes in working with diagnoses that include sensory processing challenges when this type of doctor is available in their community.

Some Resources That Might Help
(See additional resources for all age groups in *Appendix I*)

BOOKS
- *Baby Wise: Healthy Sleep Habits, Healthy Child* by Marc Weissbluth
- *Building The Bonds Of Attachment: Awakening Love in Deeply Troubled Children* by Daniel Hughes
- *First Feelings* by Stanley Greenspan and Nancy Thorndike Greenspan

- *Infant Massage: A Handbook For Loving Parents* by Vimala Schneider McClure
- *The Happiest Baby On The Block* by Harvey Karp (also available on DVD)
- *Your Baby And Child* by Penelope Leach
- *The Neurobehavioral and Social-Emotional Development Of Infants And Children* by Ed Tronick

3

Toddler Years:
What Am I Doing Wrong?

*In the toddler years, I spent a lot of time caught up in my son's "belief" that he needed certain and specific things to happen in order for him to be safe. Like having a balloon or toy be the right color, getting the same seat in the car every time, reading books in the correct order or fantasy play that followed an exacting script. And I was not the kind of mom you'd want to mess with, say, at a birthday party when the party favors were being handed out. With no regard to fairness or even very much to the feelings of the other children, I would barge through the crowd to make absolutely sure, for example, that we would walk away with the <u>red</u> (engine, car, lollipop) in our hands. Because, I justified, we **needed** it to survive...and anyway, those other kids could just go home and get a nice, long night's sleep.*

While some children demonstrate differences in their ways of learning and growing early on, remember that development in the toddler years (usually considered to be ages one to two and a half or three) is as unique and diverse as each child. Even though it might seem that there are specific times that milestones should be occurring (e.g., walking, talking or potty-training), in reality there is a huge range of "normal" in the development of young children. These differences can be easily noticed both in individual children and in comparing the development of boys and girls. Continue to notice your own reaction to your child. Are you concerned because he/she is not doing as much as the cousins or the other children at childcare? Or do you have a deep sense that something is standing in the way of your child's healthy and happy development at this stage of his/her life? Are you noticing some of the following and wondering if there is more to your family's struggles than what you are doing or not doing at home?

Things You Might Notice

1. Issues with sleep: You may notice that your toddler—
   - Still does not seem settled into any kind of sleep routine (e.g., times for going to sleep, waking up or taking naps)
   - Has inconsistent and unpredictable sleep patterns (e.g., falls asleep or wakes up unexpectedly)
   - Has trouble falling asleep
   - Has trouble staying asleep
   - Finds waking up very difficult—wakes up grumpy, dazed, unable to get going
   - May take naps that seem much too long or much too short

2. Issues with eating: The toddler might—
   • Have a hard time transitioning to solid food (e.g., is an unusually picky eater or cannot digest new foods)
   • Have strong preferences or strong avoidances for very specific tastes, temperatures or textures of food (these preferences/avoidances might also last longer than you expect in a young child)
   • Seem to want something constantly to be in his/her mouth (a breast or bottle, a pacifier, toys, blankets, clothing, etc.)
   • Continue to rely only on the breast or bottle for comfort or self-regulation
   • Have a lot of difficulty with digestion or food sensitivities or suspected allergies or food intolerances

3. Issues with comfort: You might notice that your child is —
   • Very difficult to comfort
   • Whiny, clingy or frequently crying
   • Not able to recover from "seemingly minor" upsets (e.g., huge "tantrums" over seemingly small issues)
   • Demanding more "control" than other toddlers, or conversely not requesting to do things independently (e.g., not starting to demand "I'll do it myself!")
   • Complacent, not going through the "terrible twos"
   • Unusually upset by self-care routines such as hair washing/combing or tooth brushing, bathing, dressing/undressing
   • Demonstrating very specific clothing preferences
   • Not demonstrating a typical response to the pain of falls, cuts, bumps and bruises (either over-responding or under-responding)

4. Issues with communication: Your child might—
   - Not be able to communicate his/her needs
   - Not be aware when other people are hurt or upset
   - Not be starting to use words
   - Be difficult to understand in his/her early attempts at verbal communication

5. Issues in the community: When you leave home you might notice that your child is—
   - Difficult to take to places such as restaurants, grocery stores, parties or family events
   - Highly upset by dentist appointments, doctor appointments and haircuts
   - Upset by change or transition
   - Not interested in acting independently
   - Withdrawing or separating from situations that other toddlers seem to enjoy
   - Avoidant of sensory play such as sand boxes, finger painting, water tables or swimming
   - Fearful of some playground equipment such as toddler swings or slides, or conversely requesting very high pushes or fast spins on the swings
   - Very determined to have things be one specific way (e.g., color preferences, seat at the table or order of play routines)

Trusting Your Feelings

When PJ was a toddler, he loved routines such as watching a specific show while eating a specific snack when he woke in the morning or from a nap, engaging in the exact same games or actions around bath or meal times and reading the same books in the same order before bed. While he was quite frustrated by disruptions to these specific routines, we came to realize that at the same time he seemed to need a great deal of novelty in order to engage in physical activity and stay emotionally even throughout the day. We learned for example, that when we took PJ to the same park day after day, he became unwilling to play and difficult to manage, but when we went to a different park each time, he was a much more pleasant boy for his parents and other families to spend time with. Therein began our search for all of the many parks in our community, dutifully driving him to a new play place each day. Other people thought this was a bit extreme, and we sometimes thought we were pretty crazy ourselves, but on the bright side looking back we had some very fun and compelling park adventures! Over time we learned more realistic strategies for balancing the need for routine with the need for novelty, and now, in hindsight, it is clear that there was plenty of time to figure it all out.

The toddler years are known for certain stressors, often called the "terrible twos." You might notice that your little one is demonstrating some of the expected characteristics such as tantrums in public places and loud demands for what he/she wants, but that your child's behavior and demands might be more intense. Conversely, your toddler might seem to shut down in public places, to develop play interests that set them apart from other children, or to have difficulty communicating wants and needs. These differences might be interpreted by others as reflecting poor parenting or characteristics of the child that should be changed. Allow yourself to notice what is different about your child's needs, to honor your child's unique ways of being and to slowly consider the responses and daily structure that will be most helpful for your individual family.

Dealing With Family Members and Friends

When PJ was two years old, a friend invited him for an evening at a crowded sporting event. This was something that she thoroughly enjoyed and that her own child had loved to do years earlier. I remember deciding that this was a situation that would be too hard for my boy, with intermittent loud and unfamiliar noises, bright lights, unexpected touch and intense expression of emotion. I also remember all too clearly the response to my concerns: that I was over protective, trying to shelter my little one from the world, not allowing him a "normal" life. Looking back, I know that while there was truth in this critique of my parenting, I did make many just right decisions on behalf of my son doing the best that I could with what I was learning.

Sadly, the Baby Olympics did not end with your child's first birthday. In fact, this "comparison competition" becomes even fiercer with the development of more complex behaviors and the continued emergence of language, motor and think-ing skills. Well-meaning family and friends might demand to know why you cannot control your toddler's behavior, why your toddler seems to be ruling your life, why your toddler is still nursing/drinking from a bottle/using a pacifier, why your toddler does not eat what is put on the table and, of course, why on earth your toddler does not sleep through the night in his/her own bed. Certainly, these questions can plague the life of any parent of a young child. Yet when your child has specific difficulties understanding information from touch, movement and gravity, or from hearing and seeing, his/her behaviors may truly be more extreme than those of other children. Dealing with the judgment of other people can therefore be exacerbated. You may find it even harder to cope if you are dealing with your own feelings of inadequacy and frustration.

As the parent living with your child's unique nervous system every day, you continue to have opportunities that help you better understand your child. Because you are having a different parenting experience than many others, important adult relationships may start to change or be redefined, even more than you might have expected. Perhaps by now you have met other people who share similar experiences, or you have created new friendships that support the work of parenting your exceptional little child. Your advocacy for the special needs of your toddler is important and critical work, even if your heroism is not apparent to all of the people around you!

For some specific and even humorous ideas for responding to feedback from friends and family, see *Appendix IV.*

For me, a key support was participating in a playgroup with other parents I already knew who had children of similar ages. These parents were not only also experiencing the day-to-day life of parenting young children, but we could share the differences in the development amongst our children. Though it was sometimes painful for me to see areas of advanced development in some of the other little members of the group, my grown-up playgroup friends, several of whom admittedly were also pediatric therapists, were able to appreciate some of my struggles as a mother first hand. Perhaps more importantly however, they were also able to see, and remind me of, the strengths of my own child.

Supportive Environments for Toddlers

In general, the world of a toddler should be filled with tremendous opportunities for play and socialization. Under NO circumstances should any toddler be <u>required</u> to participate in any pre-academic or academic work such as cutting, coloring, work with letters or numbers or be asked to sit still for more than one or two minutes at a time, except perhaps during mealtime.

Toddlers, especially boys, often seek a lot of rough and tumble play, and indeed this type of activity is extremely supportive for their growth and development. Toddlers need lots of experiential activities (e.g., learning through doing) and they need many opportunities to repeat and refine the things that they are learning with their bodies. In fact, children at this age will often delight in repeatedly performing their new skills. This repetition is a key to successful mastery, and while busy parents can find it hard to wait while their excited toddler climbs those stairs just one more time, it is a great gift to your little one to allow them to practice all that they are mastering with their minds and their bodies at this exciting time of life. In addition, toddlers need constant opportunities for conversation with adults and chances to listen to language being spoken around them and books being read to them, though it can be important to remember that some young children can become overwhelmed by too much verbal language. When this is the case, remember that communication involves back and forth exchanges of information – these exchanges can involve the use of facial expression and gestures as well as words. Television and computer games should be very limited for children in this age range.

That being said, toddlers also need to have clear expectations for behavior with limits and simple consequences. This not only creates order in the life of the family, it allows growing young children to feel a sense of order and safety in their expanding world. It is helpful for even very young children to be given responsibilities that they can handle (e.g., putting toys away) to support their growing independence and feelings of confidence as individuals. Some children more than others benefit from establishing early routines and habits.

All of these ideas are especially important for children who are experiencing difficulty processing the world through their senses. For one thing, while other toddlers might be able to "tolerate" expectations that are not developmentally appropriate (such as sitting still or having focused attention), children with sensory integration difficulties often literally cannot. In fact, their bodies might need more movement, more opportunities to play and explore, and they might need more time to understand their physical and social world before being ready to take on more structured demands. They may have an especially difficult time understanding words when they are distressed or upset and, similarly, have a very difficult time communicating their needs and wants. It is important that we help the people around them understand that these toddlers are not being "non-compliant," "manipulative" or "naughty" children. Rather, though they would like more than anything to succeed, they are sometimes simply not able to do what we want them to or to follow our adult rules.

Childcare

Many toddlers spend long periods of time in childcare settings; these very situations can be quite challenging for children who are having difficulty "making sense of their senses." Group childcare settings often require all children to follow specific routines, eat the same foods and be on the same sleep schedule. When these issues are still difficult at home, the adjustment away from home can be especially hard. You may hear reports of your child demonstrating aggressive behavior, or on the other hand, being extremely passive and "shut down." Your toddler might have a very hard time separating from you each day, and might also have a hard time leaving the childcare setting when it is time to go back home.

Conversely, you might get glowing reports from the childcare providers, only to find that your toddler is extremely irritable once you get home or that he/she does not want to interact with you or anyone else at the end of the day. Some children are able to hold it together when they are away from home, only showing their level of distress in the safety and comfort of their own familiar people and places. This phenomenon sometimes leads to the erroneous conclusion that the child's upset is caused by the mother or father when, in fact, it is actually a reflection of the safe relationship the little one finds within the family, the place he/she does not have to "hold it together." As stated in the infancy chapter, maintaining relationships with care providers and integrating specific strategies that are working at home will be crucial in the childcare environment.

For sample letters to important people in your child's life, see *Appendix III*.

Using Sensory Strategies At Home

While it is always exciting to find out about things that you can do at home to help your growing child manage his/her daily life, the prospect of home interventions can be overwhelming. For many of us, our lives feel very full of things to accomplish and it can be hard to imagine adding specific daily sensory activities to our already over the top to do lists. It is helpful to remember that sensory strategies should, after the initial effort to learn how to use them, be able to be integrated into everyday life and make your life easier and not harder. A long list of strategies to try at home is provided in *Appendix VI*. When children with sensory processing difficulties begin to receive the type and amount of sensory input that works for their bodies, you might find that they will be more ready to be happy and cooperative family members! That being said, you might find that helpful sensory suggestions do not seem to be enough for your challenging toddler. Sometimes this is the point that parents choose to seek professional intervention. Receiving professional guidance can better direct your selection of sensory strategies, toys or therapy equipment for your home.

When PJ was a toddler, we spent extraordinary amounts of time and energy trying to figure out how to get him up and moving. It was often exasperating to experience his seeming complete lack of motivation to initiate any type of movement while at the same time deal with his irritability and frustration when he didn't get moving! We learned over time that by taking PJ on outings to new and different places several times each day and inventing games that motivated him to move his body, we could get him to be more active and therefore later more calm and content. This strategy, while quite effective, was exhausting! After a while, we understood that we needed professional intervention. When PJ began individual occupational therapy, we were given a program that more specifically addressed his sensory needs and prescribed the frequency and intensity of input most helpful to his body.

For me, the ability to turn over these needs to someone else, and better yet someone who knew specifically what he needed, was a huge relief. I can still remember going to PJ's occupational therapy session with Carla, carrying Bob in an infant seat, and the peace of mind I experienced watching my two-year-old climbing and jumping and swinging in ways that were so hard for him to do on the playground. In therapy, PJ was able to learn how to create a "plan" with his body so that he could figure out how to do these things that he did not naturally know how to do on his own. This allowed him to feel safe and excited and more amazingly, motivated to repeat these actions over and again. For the days when we were not in therapy, I could support him to practice the many ways of moving and playing that I had not been able to teach him on my own. Thanks to Carla, I was armed with a specific plan to address his sensory processing, I was able to better and more easily provide what he needed, and ultimately share a more peaceful existence.

Considering Professional Help

The toddler years might be a time when you think about looking into the possibility of seeking sensory integration based occupational therapy intervention. Often parents decide to seek intervention when they feel they are continuing to deal with the same issues as in infancy, or they notice that their toddler still seems to need a lot of the comfort strategies discussed in the previous section. At this stage you might want more help because your toddler continues to have behaviors that seem to be out of control and are not responsive to typical behavioral strategies. Some of the largest concerns that often cause parents to seek professional help from an occupational therapist might include that the toddler:

- Still does not sleep in any predictable routine
- Has not started to eat solid foods
- Has a very limited diet and therefore is not gaining weight
- Does not seem interested in other people or has difficulty meeting new people
- Is not able to play alone
- Has difficulties being around other children
- Has difficulties being in new places or in stimulating environments (e.g., grocery stores, restaurants)
- Demonstrates motor skills behind others his/her age

Some Resources That Might Help
(Additional Resources in *Appendix I*)

BOOKS
- *Building Healthy Minds: The Six Experiences That Create Intelligence and Emotional Growth in Babies and Young Children* by Stanley Greenspan and Nancy Lewis
- *Out of the Mouths of Babes* by Shiela Frick, Ron Frick, Patricia Oetter, and Eileen Richter
- *Parenting With Love and Logic* by Foster Cline and Jim Fay
- *Playful Parenting* by Lawrence Cohen
- *Positive Discipline* by Jane Nelson
- *Positive Discipline in the First Three Years* by Jane Nelson, Cheryl Erwin, and Roslyn Ann Duffy
- *What's Going on in There? How The Brain and Mind Develop in the First Five Years of Life* by Lise Eliot

AUDIO
- *Making Sense of Sensory Integration* by Jane Koomar and Stacey Szklut (available at Future Horizons and at www.amazon.com)

COMMUNITY RESOURCES
- Developmental Swimming Programs
- Gymboree
- Kindermusic
- Playgroups

4

Preschool Years:
In Dread of Kindergarten!

When PJ was a preschooler, I worried a lot about all of the things he could not do—like climbing a ladder on the playground, getting dressed or even undressed on his own, or packing up his lunchbox at the end of the school day. And I received some pretty negative feedback from on-looking adults. The message seemed to be that, if we just had good boundaries with PJ he would simply go to his room and get dressed when told. Looking back, I realize what a waste of time and energy it was to worry about all of these things. True, PJ was not able to get dressed independently until he was eight years old, and it was many years after that before he was able to zip his jacket. But do you know what? Now he can. And all the worrying and feeling somehow "less than" other parents did not affect the timetable in which this happened one single bit. He simply could not do certain things with his body until he could.

Many people hold the child philosophy that "children would if they wanted to," but understanding sensory integration theory allows us to embrace a different idea that says, "he/she would if he/she could."

All kinds of "regular" activities just seemed to take more time, planning and effort for our family. Before a birthday party, we would have to rehearse with PJ all of the possible things that were likely to happen—such as games that might be hard for him to do with his body, food that he might not like, or loud singing around the birthday cake. Getting a haircut involved finding some kind of a prop, toy or book that related to a current passion of PJ's so he could "lose himself" in talking about the item he brought to the wonderful man who cut his hair. And as for the dentist, we needed to remember to bring our own, specific type of toothpaste and be ready to explain to the hygienist/dentist why, during his appointment, PJ needed to wear an x-ray apron (because this provided him with the calming deep touch pressure input that he needed in order to tolerate someone's hands in his mouth) even when he wasn't getting an x-ray.

The preschool years can be characterized by increased expectations of grown-ups. Certain behaviors or personality quirks that may have been considered to be cute or interesting in the first three years of life might now begin to seem unacceptable to you or other people around you. You may be continuing to struggle with some of the same issues around sleep, eating and comfort for your child that have been mentioned in previous sections. In addition, you might be having first experiences with childcare or preschool, also highlighting some of the challenges discussed in the previous sections. You might notice at this point in your child's development that you are involved in trying to achieve a monumental balance between loving and accepting your child for exactly who he/she is and getting the support that might be needed to help your child, as well as your entire family, achieve happier and more productive lives.

Things You Might Notice

As a guiding question, you can ask yourself if the differences in your child are substantially affecting the quality of his/her life or the life of the family. Do you regularly avoid doing certain activities or being with people for fear that your child will not be able to handle the situation? Does your child express disappointment or frustration about specific things that he/she is not able to do? Does your child have difficulty being around other children his/her age? Is your child showing signs of low self-esteem? Are the other children in the family negatively impacted? In addition to earlier concerns, your growing child might also:

- Become angry, fearful or upset in crowded or stimulating places
- Struggle to make or keep friends
- Have trouble enjoying play dates or birthday parties
- Seem to be fearful of things other children are not afraid of (e.g., slides at the playground or face painting at a birthday party)
- Play well alone on a playground, but stand near an adult when many children are present

- Worry excessively ("worry wart")
- Have behavior problems such as aggression or noncompliance, or demonstrate a lot of whiny/clingy behavior, or be very controlling or directing
- Have a high activity level that at times seems out of control, or have a low activity level
- Seem to lack inhibition or self-control
- Seem to be extremely inflexible
- Hurt younger siblings or family pets (often unintentionally)
- Become very picky about clothing
- Dislike playing with things that are messy
- Have a great deal of difficulty at the dentist, doctor or haircutters
- Have trouble with potty training
- Continue to rely heavily on a pacifier, bottle or breast
- Continue to need daily naps
- Have trouble with learning self-care
- Fall, crash into things or people, or break things (a.k.a. "the bull in the china shop!")
- Seem to not notice the feeling of things such as having a shoe full of sand or clothes twisted on his/her body
- Take a lot of risks with his/her body without seeming to be afraid
- Seem to be fearful of movement (i.e., when swimming, at the playground, at an amusement park, etc.)
- Say speech sounds in a way that is hard to understand
- Have a hard time following verbal directions
- Have difficulties communicating wants and needs

- Have a hard time taking turns in play or conversation with others
- Not be putting words together in increasingly complex ways

Remember that all children will demonstrate some of the characteristics highlighted here at certain times under specific circumstances; ask yourself if you are noticing a pattern of concern and if the behaviors that you are observing are creating actual difficulty in your life or the life of your child. When you are deciding whether or not it is time to seek professional guidance, you may want to ask yourself if your child is showing frequent frustration and/or avoidance of activities in which other children are readily engaging and enjoying. Each child has distinct preferences for play activities and social engagement, but if your child seems to be significantly more limited in choices and preferences than others, it may be a sign of needing help due to a possible diagnosis of Sensory Processing Disorder.

Trusting Your Feelings

*In the preschool years it is ironic how it can already start to feel like time is running out. This is certainly even truer today than it was when I was in this stage with PJ in 1995, given growing demands for early developing academics and behavioral control. Still, I remember the feeling that the clock was ticking, and pretty soon he would be expected to be ready for **kindergarten**—a place where his little square peg would have to start molding into that dreaded round hole.*

Remember that these preschool years are special and unique in and of themselves, and not simply a dry run for life in kindergarten and beyond. Children do not need to "practice" behaviors that they are not developmentally ready for in order to perform them some day in the future. **For children with sensory processing problems, it is particularly important for adults to understand that repeatedly trying to do things that they are not ready to do with their bodies, or are unable to make sense of with their brains, will only further disorganize their growing nervous systems. This makes the possibility for success less, and not more, likely in the future.** The gift of time to learn is one of the greatest gifts we can give our children, and still, this might be the stage that you feel you need to find some more specific intervention for your child.

By the time children are in preschool, if they are not performing in ways that society expects them to perform, everyone starts to look for someone to blame. For people outside the family, the likely candidates are the parents. For the parents, it might be teachers, relatives or perhaps one another. For the children, even at this early age, they begin to suspect that the blame falls with them. In reality, when children have difficulty making sense of the information coming in through their senses, the "fault" lies with a difference in their central nervous system that creates a tangle in sensory processing. As parents, we have a lot of power to call a halt to the blaming, in part by freely acknowledging that our children came into the world with some difficulties, as well as gifts, and also by positively enlisting the support of others as we seek constructive solutions to assist our children to have the best possible quality of life.

In the months before the big transition to kindergarten, PJ joined a summer "Friendship Group" with Carla at KidPower Therapy Associates in Albuquerque. The friendship group was based on the "How Does Your Engine Run"® Alert Program® (Williams & Shellenberger, 1996) and was designed to teach self-regulation as well as social skills to a group of five young children, each getting ready to make the big step to kindergarten that coming fall. This was an amazing group and we saw our children grow profoundly in their understanding of their own bodies and minds, learning strategies to support their attention and behavior that were immediately practiced in social interaction. At the end of the summer, neither parents nor children were ready to let go of their friendship group; the unfortunate enthusiastic therapists found themselves stuck with us for the next nine months! Over this time, the children continued to develop self-regulation, with the focus creatively designed to support needed school-related skills. Sessions included trips to local schools, indoor playgrounds, and one another's birthday parties. A highlight of this remarkable experience was an evening trip to Albuquerque's International Balloon Fiesta. Many of the children had previously found this annual event to be difficult because of the crowded park, the loud roar of the burners and the intense visual stimulation of fire and color.

That fall evening, the friendship group gathered on the balloon field with parents and siblings. The children were armed with fanny packs filled with chosen items to help them feel comfortable and safe, such as gum, things to suck on, hats with bills, earplugs and sunglasses...all strategies the children had learned and practiced in the Alert Program® component of the friendship group. One ingenious father even cut the headphones from the stereo to protect his boy from the noise! They were bolstered by the plans (pictures) they each carried to help them remember what they needed, and uplifted by the support and caring of their group leaders and of one another. I will never forget the feeling of watching my little boy and his friends participate in this community event. Anyone who looked closely would have recognized that there were some differences between this group of children and other children, but no one would have doubted for a minute that they were exactly where they belonged. It is this feeling that is so difficult to communicate, because it is born of the magic of the therapeutic process but also of the peace of acceptance and appreciation.

If I could whisper in the ear of my younger self, I would tell her to breathe this acceptance and appreciation deeply, to give rest to fear of the future and, with the help of all the wonderful and necessary professionals, try hard to enjoy each moment of the incredible journey.

Supportive Environments for Preschool Aged Children

Preschool aged children continue to need plenty of opportunities to move and engage in play that allows them to use their muscles intensely. They might be ready now for short periods of focused attention, but much of their learning should still be self-directed and very physically active. Some three-, four- and five- year olds will enjoy cutting, drawing and coloring, and some preschoolers might show an interest in pre-academic activities such as learning letters and numbers or writing their names. While it is important to encourage these interests, it is not necessary for future learning to begin practicing these skills at this time. Preschoolers also continue to need plenty of opportunities for conversation with adults, and they are often ready at this age to engage meaningfully with other children. Pretend play is an extraordinary aspect of thinking and language development at this time of life, so they need to have lots of life experiences and then encouragement, props and time to play out their daily adventures in the pretend world. At this age children love to practice all of the things they are learning; they need time and repetition to refine all of their exploding motor, social and language skills. They are also learning about their feelings and the feelings of others. When adults label emotions and provide empathy about a variety of feelings, we are engaging in some of the most important work of the preschool years.

The environment, while providing spaces and places for lots of physical play, also needs to include quiet places where children can "get away" from sensory stimulation and social interaction when they need to. Occupational therapists Patti Oetter and Eileen Richter coined the term "womb space" to describe quiet spaces that mimic the sensory qualities of the actual womb — dark, quiet, and warm with opportunities for deep pressure touch (Richter & Oetter, 1990, p. 3-4). Parents and teachers have created these spaces using free-standing tents, blankets over tables, pillows and stuffed animals. Children might create these spaces for themselves by playing under the bed or in closets, or by having more fun playing in big boxes than with the exciting thing that might have been packaged inside!

Childcare/Preschool

All of the issues around having a toddler in childcare continue to be relevant during the preschool years. In addition, growing demands for academic performance at earlier ages might make preschool an even greater challenge. While all children in the preschool years continue to need an environment that provides primarily social interaction, language, and movement play, children with sensory integration difficulties might find it even harder to deal with requirements for structure. They might have little interest in starting to use school related tools such as crayons, pencils or scissors. It can be very hard for them to stay with the group or to stay with one task for any length of time or, conversely, they may become totally absorbed in one activity or internal idea and have a hard time making a group transition. Circle time, a typical preschool activity where all of the children sit together to listen to stories or play games, can be especially difficult because of the requirements to be still for a length of time and/or the need to sit close to other children, which makes it difficult for them to predict what their peers might do next.

If you are having concerns about your child's time outside of your home (in preschool or childcare), it will be important to look closely at the sensory environment. In addition to noticing opportunities for movement and physical play, could a preschool situation be over-stimulating because of too many children, too much language or noise, or too much clutter of materials and activities in the classroom? Perhaps adjustments to the environment will be helpful, or perhaps it is time to look for a different preschool environment that will be a better match for your little one.

Much adult support continues to be necessary to facilitate growth and development for preschoolers. It is our belief that we are living in a time when unrealistic expectations in the lives of preschoolers are contributing to a mismatch between what children are doing and what we want them to do, such as having to sit too long in circle time or at table work activities or having to be still and quiet for too long. Is your child experiencing difficulties processing information from his/her senses and therefore unable to be successful in the preschool environment? Is your child "coping" with an environment that is not developmentally appropriate and therefore experiencing difficulty? Or is your child, like many others, living a combination of these situations; that is, he/she may have sensory integration difficulties but these are compounded by unrealistic expectations for any child of his/her age? Our children with sensory processing difficulties can help lead the movement to bring back developmentally appropriate practice to the lives of all young children!

When PJ was a three-year-old in preschool, he was obsessively involved with an interest in music, especially the guitar. We began to notice that when he was anxious or uncomfortable, he would strum on things as if they were a guitar, seeming to enter into a dream world of his own. One day, when I was the parent-aide in PJ's preschool classroom, the class was called to "Big

*Group" time. I noticed right away that PJ sat a little apart from the group, never wanting to be too physically close to the other children. When the teacher announced that they were going to do rock and roll dancing, an activity that would bring lots of unpredictable movement and sound, PJ moved even farther away from the group, picking up a block from the shelf on the wall and beginning to strum. As my mother heart was sinking with sadness and with fear, I heard the teacher say this: "Okay, who wants to be a dancer and who wants to play the block guitar?" And just like that, a few kids, not many but still three or four, went over to the shelf to get a block, and without being given any direction sat in a circle around PJ. I watched in amazement, realizing that of course the other kids knew that PJ was different, and of course they already knew about the strumming and the guitars. And in that moment, with the guidance of a brilliant and compassionate teacher, I experienced the first of many such lessons, **understanding little by little that the important thing for my son was not to be the same as the others, but to be a part of the others. To belong.***

Using Sensory Strategies At Home

During the preschool years, you may be concerned about skills that your son or daughter is not acquiring such as dressing, cutting or beginning to hold a pencil. While the lack of skill development can certainly indicate meaningful concerns, from a sensory perspective it will be most important to continue to provide many sensory activities that are fun and that support your child to be at his/her best at home. As stated earlier, a sample of specific strategy ideas for use at home are provided in **Appendix VI**. Some families might begin to consider the use of physical games and activities as a regular part of their daily schedule (e.g., wrestling before bedtime, jumping into pillows on the floor first thing in the morning or "crashing" into the couch before mealtime). While the addition of activity time in the home might feel strange at first, these sensory games can ease situations that are difficult such as waking up in the morning or from a nap, making transitions from one thing to another, or sitting down for family meals. One ambitious family that we knew actually purchased exercise balls in various sizes for every member of the family to sit on at the table during dinner-time. This colorful and active addition to mealtime helped them to create a way for *everyone* to be social and participatory in this important evening activity! Of course, it will be important to take into account the sensory needs of all the family members; that is, you will only be able to introduce sensory strategies that can be comfortable to everyone who is living with your child.

Considering Professional Help

Beginning to pursue professional help during the preschool years can be another tricky time for you personally. Family and friends might suggest that you are overreacting to your young child's behaviors or that you are simply not using good parenting strategies to get your child "under control." These might be the first of many experiences where being an advocate for your son or daughter means, at times, flying in the face of what other people think and continuing to do what you know inside yourself is right for your child. As parents, your most important job is to help your child maintain a sense of personal esteem—to feel that he/she is indeed successful at being a child. Surrounding yourself with people—both in the professional world and in your personal life—that will help to support that goal is one of the most important things you can do for yourself and your family.

Professional Testing and Diagnosis

Because the preschool years have typically been a time for children to be moving out into the world, it is also a time when many children are referred for testing. The suggestion that your child might have a problem is extremely difficult for any parent, and it is scary to enter into the referral process. Reports and interpretations that can be hard to understand or seem highly impersonal may add to your sense of sadness and frustration. On the other hand, it can be a relief to begin to acknowledge, more fully and more publicly, what you may have been feeling for a long time.

Ironically, when a therapist friend suggested that PJ receive testing through our public schools I was at first alarmed. While he had been receiving private occupational therapy with Carla since he was a toddler, the idea of moving into a complete evaluation through the special education system felt like a further step of acknowledging our concerns. It helped greatly to be reminded that our goal for this assessment was to have access to appropriate intervention by professionals who could help ensure his success.

Beyond the testing and the labels and the intervention, you will be starting to develop a team of people who will travel on this path with you and your child. Though you might not have expected or wanted to be on this journey, you will be amazed by the relationships you will find as you go, and the many, many extraordinary people who will become dear to you in ways you could never have imagined.

PUBLIC SCHOOLS

When seeking professional help to support sensory integration during the preschool years, you might be referred to your public school special education preschool program. You may be able to receive just the help you are looking for in a public school program. However, the federal public law, which mandates that occupational therapy services (as well as speech-language and physical therapy) be offered by the public schools to children ages three to 21, only refers to "educationally related difficulties." In this way, school-based therapists might assess and intervene only with problems involving specific skills needed for success in the preschool environment, such as improved perceptual skills for learning shapes and colors, or improved fine motor skills for cutting or drawing. Interpretation of this law may vary from district to district. Two helpful resources for understanding public school law related to Sensory Processing Disorder are *Sensational Kids* (Miller, 2007) and *Parenting a Child with Sensory Processing Disorder* (Auer, 2006) — see **Appendix I**. Some children with sensory integration difficulties might not be eligible for therapy services through the educational system because their areas of need may not be considered directly related to pre-academic skill development.

PRIVATE PRACTITIONERS

A more clinical approach to assessment and therapy is done by private occupational therapists who consider the sensory foundations underlying the specific difficulties your child might be having at home or in the community. If you feel your child might benefit from sensory integration therapy, begin by talking to your child's doctor, teachers or other parents that you know, or by looking in the phonebook under "Occupational Therapy" or on-line by searching "Sensory Processing Disorder." There are many multi-sensory programs that are not based on the principles of sensory integration therapy as developed by Dr. Ayres, therefore, it will be important for you to research, ask questions and seek a clinic that provides this specific therapy implemented by a qualified and experienced occupational therapist.

Some Resources That Might Help
(Additional Resources in *Appendix I*)

BOOKS
- *Love & Logic Solutions For Kids With Special Needs* by David Funk
- *SenseAbilities: Understanding Sensory Integration* by Maryann Colby Trott, Marci Laurel, & Susan Windeck
- *Skillstreaming in Early Childhood: New Strategies and Perspectives for Teaching Prosocial Skills* by Ellen McGinnis and Arnold Paul Goldstein
- *The Explosive Child: A New Approach for Understanding and Parenting Easily Frustrated, Chronically Inflexible Children* by Ross W. Greene

- *Pathways to Play! Combining Sensory Integration and Integrated Play Groups* by Glenda Fuge and Rebecca Berry
- *The Challenging Child: Understanding, Raising, and Enjoying the Five "Difficult" Types of Children* by Stanley I. Greenspan

DVD

- *Sensory Processing for Parents: From Roots to Wings* by Judith E. Reisman

COMMUNITY

- Developmentally Oriented Dance Classes
- Preschool Gymnastics
- Swimming

5

Elementary School: Standing In Line, Paying Attention, Homework And Science Fair...

It can be challenging to maintain perspective while writing about the school years. How do I describe the exhilaration of success, the devastation of failure? The comparisons generated once school starts make the "Baby Olympics" seem, pardon the pun, like child's play. Now the gaps in performance between my children and other children were literally hanging on the walls, they were visible on desks and tables, they were everywhere I turned.

Yet, the help our family received to allow for success in these school years was extraordinary. It would take too many pages to express my gratitude, love even, for all of the wonderful educators who became a part of our world. But that gratitude, that love, it cost me each day. It meant that I lived in need of these other people, that I had to nurture relationships with them, that

I had to care about what they thought and what they understood about my sons. At times, it was exhausting.

Having my sons be successful in school meant that I was in school too, because these two courageous and imaginative boys could not do school on their own. They needed sensory help for self-regulation and focus, they needed logistical help for planning and organization, they needed emotional help to keep on trying and they needed hands on help to literally complete the work that was required. School was teamwork at our house, and at some times the team functioned better than at others!

Over time what I learned to understand was that even though providing all of this help felt hard sometimes, it was essentially okay, because I didn't have to play the comparison game when I could just stop participating in it. And the relationships that I worked so hard to maintain were a gift that I would not have had in my life if it were not for the special needs of my children. And finally, whatever help the boys needed to make it through was just what I was here to do one day at a time. When I could stop being afraid and when I could stop thinking that they "shouldn't" still be needing this much help, I was able to appreciate the opportunity that we were given in our unique family to work closely together day by day.

Now that you have arrived at the school years, you probably have a mixture of emotions. Your child has grown in a variety of ways, perhaps demonstrating some tenacity and courage that you have admired. On the other hand, your elementary school-aged child might not seem ready for the challenges that lie ahead, or might already be struggling to be successful academically, behaviorally and/or socially. You might find that the elementary school environment is not as forgiving of your child's differences as was the early childhood setting. You might also, once again, feel you are being judged as a parent, this time because school is not going smoothly for your child. Now, more than ever, your job as a parent is to continue supporting your son or daughter in every way you know how. This job is critically important. Your yardstick for success might not be grades or certificates of achievement, rather you must consider your child's self-esteem as a primary goal for all of the coming years. Communicating this overriding goal with the school staff will become a crucial aspect of your relationships at school.

I recently came across a short piece I wrote when Carla and I were teaching in the early 2000s that describes how I was feeling at this time in our lives when starting a new school year was so challenging.

BACK TO SCHOOL

It's July again, and as sure as the soaring heat and the long days of light, I marvel at the peace in my heart about my children. Kids who today seem to me clever, creative, fun loving, okay. Yet as the days move forward, anxiety starts to creep in with the specter of school looming closer. How is it, I ask myself, that these same two children, so lovely in summer, become somehow wrong, even deficient at the start of the school year? When spontaneity becomes difficulty with structure, imagination transforms into lack of focus, free thinking makes way for mandated tasks, pretend play goes under to homework that must be completed.

And how, I ask myself, can I keep peace in my heart, when skills lag behind peers, when effort is questioned, when the extraordinary energy required to meet school demands takes a visible toll on physical, emotional and spiritual well-being?

Sometimes I want to take flight, say "no more," we will just stay in perpetual summer. But here is what is true. My job as a parent is to work to know, every minute, that my children are really okay. To see them in appreciation of who they are, and not in fear of who they are not. This is my biggest job, my most important challenge. I resolve to attend actively to this pursuit as we move into the new year. And I ask that all of the wonderful therapists and teachers in our lives would help me to remember this simple truth – in all four seasons.

Things You Might Notice

Many of the characteristics of sensory integration challenges that have been discussed in the previous sections might still apply to your child. Now that you are dealing with school expectations, you might also notice or hear feedback from school staff about difficulties with:

- Complaints about clothes feeling uncomfortable
- Hygiene (e.g., regular bathing, teeth brushing and hair care)
- Self-help skills

- Impulsivity
- Unpredictable outbursts
- Overly aggressive or controlling behavior toward peers
- Withdrawn behavior with peers
- Understanding personal space or boundaries
- Understanding social situations or reading social cues
- Making friends and keeping friends
- Doing group work
- Group transitions such as recess, lunch or movement to special classes
- Participating in group or individual physical activities (such as PE, swimming lessons, gymnastics or dance classes) or sensory stimulating activities such as music or art
- Times of day that are less structured (e.g., self-selection or recess) or times of the day that are more structured (e.g., reading groups, math seatwork, spelling tests)
- Inconsistent performance in activities or tasks from day to day
- "Falling apart" after school (even after reports of a good day at school)
- Fidgeting with things in the desk or putting inappropriate things in his/her mouth, even though these actions might be your child's best attempt to remain focused for learning
- Ability to sit still or stay in a chair, or sit upright in the chair (e.g., child lays over the desk)
- Attention (your child may not be able to pay attention in class or he/she might have trouble showing attention by sitting up in the chair and/or looking at the teacher)
- Daydreaming during class

- Ability to focus on paper and pencil tasks
- Fatigue when doing focused work
- Anger, frustration and/or avoidance of school tasks (at school or at home)
- School skills (reading, writing and math) lagging behind peers
- Recognizing alphabet letters
- Ability to formulate letters for legible handwriting
- Formulating thoughts in words or on paper
- Showing verbally or in writing what <u>you</u> know your child knows
- Understanding time and space concepts
- Understanding expectations
- Working independently
- Organization of paperwork
- Keeping track of materials or losing materials that are expected to be transferred between home and school
- Following multi-part directions
- Story comprehension
- Vocabulary development
- Ability to hear the difference between different spoken sounds (e.g., "f" sounds like "th")
- Understanding sound-letter relationships
- Low self-esteem

Realizing that our second son, Bob, had a substantial reading disability was really a bummer. Having been pretty success-ful in my second try at the Baby Olympics, I could not help but secretly feel that I had redeemed myself in the eyes of the "judges," and here I found myself cut right back down to size. Even though I knew it didn't make sense, I felt some personal shame about having another child who was not "developing normally." And, besides, was I supposed to learn all about reading problems now? I simply didn't have time for this new turn of events!

One thing I discovered right away was that while "sensory integration dysfunction" seemed to arouse interest and empathy in most school personnel, not learning to read was a much more serious offense. Living in times when all children are supposed to be at or above average in their reading skills, the non-reader finds himself at odds with the very system in which he is trying to succeed. He is, according to some ways of thinking, the living proof that the school system is not performing adequately. And even though the problem is inside him—his brain, his eyes, his capacity to learn— the system is set up to defend itself and sometimes it reverts to trying to find someone else to blame. Sometimes, even, to wanting to put distance between itself and the non-reading child.

I have to laugh now when I think of the angst we experienced when Bob could not read a single word at the age of seven. In reality, reading did not start to happen until much, much later and then only with very intensive intervention by outstanding professionals. Perhaps if we had had a crystal ball, we could have understood that the most important thing we could do for our son was to help him to stop defining his success as a learner and as a child by his ability to read, write and be organized at school. Luckily, he found a teacher, mentor and friend who was able to give him that essential gift.

Trusting Your Feelings

Now that your child is in a school community, you may find that there seems to be some kind of a mismatch between what you know your child is capable of, who you know your child is inside, and what he/she is actually able to show in the school setting each day. This is a pivotal time to be clear that the things you know about your son or daughter, born of a lifetime of living with them and loving them, are true and real and important. This is the time when you might have to ask yourself what it actually means to be a "successful" child. While all parents want their children to perform well in school, school performance is not what defines a child as okay or special. A child's school performance is not a gauge of a good or competent parent either!

The school years are also a time when you might need to learn to "listen" more carefully to your child than ever before. Sometimes your child will tell you with words what he/she is wanting, needing or experiencing at school. At other times he/she might show you with difficult behaviors that may be more challenging to interpret. If you have a sense that a negative behavior is a sign of distress or a cry for help rather than a purposeful manipulation, then it probably is. Children with Sensory Processing Disorder sometimes have no other way to show what they are experiencing inside. The more you practice consistent parenting skills, the more easily you will be able to distinguish between purposeful behavior and sensory processing differences. Once again, you get the job of advocating for your child even when many other people do not agree with your point of view.

I remember when Bob was a struggling second grader and we started getting feedback that our usually compliant seven-year-old would not follow simple directions, such as wearing his coat to walk across the school campus. Initially we tried to talk to him about this "behavior" and then to apply consequences for negative reports from school. Eventually, however, we came to understand that this behavior was a reaction to intense anger and frustration resulting from what seemed a total inability to be successful at school. Later he was able to verbalize what it felt like to simply be too angry to follow a direction that did not make sense to him, just to please an adult with whom he associated so much failure.

Supportive Environments for Elementary School Aged Children

Many of the aspects of supportive environments discussed earlier relating to younger children still apply to your school-aged child. Children in elementary school continue to need frequent opportunities for movement, conversation and hands-on learning. As they get older, they will have a longer attention span and an increasing ability to do focused work, but will need sensory input to support thinking and learning throughout life.

As you become more and more dependent on people outside of your family to support your child's progress and happiness at school and in the community, you will begin to notice that some adults are a better match for your child than others. It is important to acknowledge that the needs of a child with Sensory Processing Disorder can be different or more intense than the needs of other children. This means that finding teachers and other adults who are a good fit for your child is essential. It is very important, in the spirit of teamwork, that this match be made without blaming or judgment. When you can take responsibility for your child's differences (e.g., "Johnny really needs a place where he can make noise and move around" or "Carol needs a quiet classroom that is structured and focused"), you show respect for the school and community support staff while advocating at the same time for your child's needs. Remember that most adults (classroom teachers, PE teachers, coaches etc.), usually without even realizing, will create an environment that most closely matches their own sensory needs (e.g., quiet vs. noisy, visually stimulating vs. stark, or structured vs. free flowing). Sometimes just explaining the reasons why your child needs modifications to the environment or the classroom rules might help a teacher to be comfortable with making these adjustments for your child. On the other hand, it would be just as unreasonable to expect a teacher to manage what he/she might feel as a barrage of sensory input, such as a child moving around in the back of the classroom, if this does not match the needs of that particular teacher's nervous system that requires structure and order. It is a great step toward collaboration and teamwork when all of the members of the team can acknowledge their own learning/working style without judgment or blame.

SCHOOL ENVIRONMENT

In general it is a good practice to start looking for a classroom in the spring prior to fall enrollment. Assessing whether a classroom and a teacher might be a good fit is often best accomplished through direct observation. There are multiple criteria to consider. You will want to notice the physical environment, the style of the teacher(s) and the overall classroom schedule. However, also remember to keep in mind the time of the school year that you are observing. If it is toward the end of the school year, the children have already grown up and learned a lot and will be doing things your child would not be expected to do at the start of the next school year. In addition, it can be helpful to look for a child in the classroom who reminds you of your own son or daughter. How does the teacher respond to that child and how is the teacher able to deal with that child's special needs? In some schools, you will find resistance to the idea of "shopping" for a classroom for your child. While the administration may have valid reasons for limiting this practice, you might find that they are more open to your need to observe when you explain your special circumstances, emphasizing the need to find a good match for your child without judging the overall competence of any of the teachers in the building. If you still are not allowed to observe, this might be a time to consider whether this is going to be a workable school environment for your family.

NON-SCHOOL ENVIRONMENTS
Of course, your child is also continuing his/her life outside of school! While it can be especially important not to over-structure the lives of children who may desperately need down time after the demands of the school day, some community activities can be particularly helpful for children with sensory processing difficulties. These might include: bike riding, bowling, dancing, gymnastics, music lessons, horseback riding, martial arts, hiking, rock climbing, skating, skiing, skate boarding,

swimming, track, weightlifting or yoga. Once you have learned about the types of sensory input that are organizing for your child, you can seek out community activities that provide these types of input as a regular part of his/her life. The same characteristics that you would look for in a school environment and teacher are good guidelines for choosing community activities. Often the best way to find a good match is by talking to other parents who are dealing with similar challenges.

Many children with sensory processing difficulties have a challenging time with team oriented sports. This can be related to having to deal with all the other children moving around them, the large area of the playing space, the lines and boundaries and goals, the rules, and/or the social skills, not to mention the potential for managing a bat, racquet or moving ball! These children tend to respond better and develop more competence at individual activities and sports (e.g., swimming or track) where their bodies can move and develop skills at their own pace, and with less direct effect of their own performance on the rest of the team.

Considering Professional Help

PROFESSIONAL TESTING AND DIAGNOSIS
While you may have experienced the process of testing and diagnosis before your child got to school, many children are not identified as having problems until they are already "failing" at school. It is a sad statement about our educational relationship to children that so many children experience school as a place where they cannot be successful no matter how much they

want to be or how hard they try. When you are contacted by the school to initiate the process of testing, you might have a variety of reactions. Perhaps you might be angry and frustrated that your child is being labeled and categorized—and you may be afraid that a special education label will be detrimental to your child. Or you might be relieved that someone else is noticing what you have seen for a long time, perhaps hopeful that your child will receive services that can help.

The testing and eligibility process may be long and painful. It is never easy to think or talk about the things that your child does not do well. In addition, standardized tests can never describe your child to you—a test cannot address, for example, his/her caring for people, love of nature, passions for certain ideas or spirit of adventure. Try to remember that testing is simply intended to provide more information about your child's academic performance and needs. Once these are well defined, a plan should be developed and specific support services identified to meet those needs.

It is essential for you to have allies during this difficult process. Try to bring a supportive family member or friend to meetings where your child's problems will be discussed—having someone else who really knows your little person can keep you feeling whole and will also give you someone to talk to later without having to re-tell the story of the meeting. In the absence of an available friend, parent advocacy groups found in most communities can also offer support. Also, remember that the school personnel, while busy and sometimes stressed, really want to do the best job they can for your family. Do not hesitate to remind them that you want to hear positive things about your child as well as interpretations of the schools' concerns. Asking if the discussion could start with strengths might lead the meeting in a more positive direction while generating ideas and strategies.

Most of our experiences with school teams were positive ones, but I will always remember one meeting—when the significance of Bob's problems at school was first being identified—where not one single positive thing was said by his teacher about our son. It is hard to describe the vulnerability of a parent in such a situation; for me, it was as if my heart was sitting out, exposed on the table, and I desperately needed everyone in the room to be careful with it. I later learned that I needed to ask for this care— by creating relationships with all the members of the team and by asking directly during each meeting for whatever would help me to stay present and positive. Usually, this can happen in a spirit of mutual respect and caring, but occasionally, it meant setting boundaries about what was not acceptable to us as parents.

It is also important to understand that school-based personnel may or may not have much information about and/or experience with Sensory Processing Disorder. You may find yourself in the role of educating the school team about the issues that are relevant to your child right at the start of the testing process. For example, does your child need frequent movement or heavy work breaks in order to perform optimally during standardized testing? Would something to chew on help? Does the evaluator need to be aware of certain behaviors that might emerge during testing when your child is required to be still and focused for a long period of time? What are your child's strengths and interests? While the professionals you are beginning to work with have a great deal of expertise related to education or therapy, you are the <u>absolute expert</u> on your child. You may find you need to develop skills that will help you organize and lead a team of professionals to help your child have the most successful school experience possible.

When I was preparing PJ for his initial evaluation with the public school team, I told him that the evaluators were interested in finding out what he was good at and what was hard for him. At that point in his life, his great passion was trains. After hours of testing, much of which was indeed challenging, we got back into the car. When I checked in with PJ about how it had gone for him, he expressed confusion. If the evaluators wanted to know what he was good at, he asked, "Why didn't they ask me about trains?"

SCHOOL-BASED SUPPORT SERVICES

As discussed in the preschool chapter, you may be able to get therapy services (such as occupational therapy) through your public school system in order to support many of your concerns. Remember, however, that some sensory related issues (such as attention difficulties, behavior problems or lack of organization) may not be considered to be directly related to classroom success and therefore your child might not qualify for school-based occupational therapy services. This can be quite confusing when these difficulties are clearly impacting your child; however, the federal public law provides occupational therapy services only for "educationally related difficulties." This means that occupational therapy might be provided in school to address specific skills, such as perceptual and fine motor skills for handwriting, but might not address sensory motor foundation skills if they are not seen as having a direct academic impact. In addition, some occupational therapists working in school settings do not have specific training in the assessment and treatment of Sensory Processing Disorder. In these cases, you might need to provide information to the educational team to help them understand your child's specific sensory issues.

While your child may not be able to receive direct treatment for sensory integration difficulties at school, try to enlist the support of your school-based occupational therapist to design modifications that will allow your child to demonstrate the best performance possible at school each day. Some examples might be: opportunities for movement at various times throughout the day, modified or reduced assignments based on specific needs, preferential seating, opportunities for multi-sensory learning and using a variety of ways to demonstrate knowledge such as dictation or keyboarding (See *Appendix VI* for more suggestions). Again, you might want to consider accessing additional direct clinical therapy services in your community for support of sensory processing concerns.

PRIVATE PRACTITIONERS

If you are thinking about pursuing direct clinical therapy services in your community it will be important to identify practitioners with expertise in Sensory Processing Disorder. You may ask your school personnel or pediatrician for referral sources, although many families find that talking to other parents and researching on the internet are most productive. As you have been learning to understand Sensory Processing Disorder and its related challenges for your child, you may now feel you know more about what questions to ask and what supports you need for home and school. Each community is different. You may find professionals with tremendous expertise in sensory integration; conversely the therapists you identify may not have this specific training. In these situations you might find yourself traveling a distance to access services and/or working together with practitioners in your community to help them understand your child's needs and potential interventions.

Some families have found that including their clinic based occupational therapist in school team meetings can help the family members articulate concerns or problem solve challenges at school. For example, one child we know struggled with the first half hour at school. The clinic based occupational therapist was able to help the family and school come up with some sensory-based activities to do before school that prepared him for that transition from home to school each day.

Creating School Teams That Work

Our first evaluation with PJ in the public preschool special education program was a difficult experience. Being "in the field" as a speech-language pathologist, I had some sense that I wanted to be part of the planning and implementation of PJ's first multi-disciplinary evaluation, but I didn't really know how to make it happen. The professionals seemed confused by my desire to talk about the type of environment and testing that I thought would work best for PJ. I was encouraged to leave the room during testing and, during the short parent interview, I was left with the impression that my answers to their posed questions were somehow wrong. For example, when I explained that my four-year-old could neither dress nor even undress himself, I was met with the reply that if I gave him enough time and expected him to do it, then he simply would.

While many professionals worked with my son over two days, only one was available to provide the interpretation of the information. This discussion felt cold and confusing; my husband Jack commented as we walked away from that meeting that he might have preferred to be hit over the head with a baseball bat! This was the beginning of our evolution as parents in understanding more fully the role we had to play as team members and even leaders. Little by little, we were able to help grow dynamic, supportive, proactive school teams, first for PJ and later for Bob. This experience of teamwork with so many extraordinary professionals has turned out to be a true enrichment in our lives.

The first step in creating a working school team is to get solidly grounded in the concept of "team." The team consists of all the people who are helping your child at school along with all of the family members who are able to be involved. **The team should have as its guiding purpose the quality of life of your child at school.** While you are the expert about your child, the team brings you a wealth of expertise as well as experience and knowledge about him/her. Sometimes you will agree with the members of your team and sometimes you will have different points of view. Mutual respect and good communication are essential.

Working on school teams means that, as a parent, you will be creating relationships with a lot of people you may not originally have been very interested in knowing! Relationships take attention and ongoing effort, and at times you may find this work to be exhausting. On the other hand, you will have a chance to work closely with, and indeed come to care deeply for, some amazing people. It is important to realize that while you are focused only on the team involving your own child, the professionals are working on many—usually too many—teams to support countless children throughout the school. The team will never mean to them what it does to you, but by practicing good communication and social interaction skills, you may be surprised how you can pull a group together!

Your school team will likely be made up of several people. Often there is a head special education teacher who has the responsibility of knowing about the programs that are available in the school and might also be the facilitator of the meeting. There might be an Individualized Education Plan (IEP) specialist who has the job of making sure the IEP is completed according to the law. There will always be an administrative designee (e.g., a principal, head teacher or district representative), a general education teacher, a member of the special education staff and related service providers such as the occupational therapist, speech-language pathologist, physical therapist and/or social worker when relevant. All of these professionals will bring expertise to the table, and yet as the parent you are the obvious expert about your specific child and may therefore wish to take the role of leader on your child's team. The leadership of your team is a hard job. Often, you will have the help and support of the school personnel—sometimes another member of the team may even be ready, willing and able to share the job with you. Whatever the configuration, nine times out of ten everyone involved wants the best possible outcome for your son or daughter. By removing roadblocks related to interpersonal communication and helping to keep the team focused on success, you will be part of creating something meaningful and important both in your life and in the life of your child.

Educators are pretty much always overworked and under-appreciated. One of the greatest things you can do on behalf of your child is to provide support to the members of your team. This can be in the form of giving time in the classroom, bringing materials that will help your child and also other children in the classroom, or sharing information about the best way to work with a child like yours in the spirit of teamwork and cooperation. It is also important to take time to appreciate all that the educators on your team do each day. This can be verbal appreciation, notes, and especially communication with supervisors of the team, letting the work that is being done on behalf of your child be publicly known.

You may have to resist the temptation to ally with one team member against another, or particularly when a situation is stressful, to look for someone else to blame. In order to provide the best possible leadership for your team, you have to be able to rise above interpersonal conflicts and hurt feelings and keep the focus on the well-being of your child. The following are some suggestions for the care and maintenance of a positive and productive school team.

Some "Dos & Don'ts" For Leading A School Team

DON'T VENT AT SCHOOL...DO VENT AT HOME!
There is probably no way to get through your experiences traversing the school world (or almost anything else in life, for that matter) without some feelings of frustration and anger. For one thing, whenever your child is struggling, you will feel at least some hurt and worry, and these can easily translate into negative feelings about the environment and/or people that comprise your child's school day. In addition, in any team situation, there will be conflict and differences of opinion. Because you are trying so hard to be a good and faithful leader of your child's school team, it is critically important to resist the temptation to vent your feelings to anyone within the school setting. This self-control will be rewarded over and over again as a trusting relationship builds between you and the school community.

It is, however, essential that you have a trusted person outside with whom to share all of your negative emotions! When you get feedback about your child that hurts your feelings, when your child is asked to do things it does not seem he/she will be able to do, when expectations at school do not seem to you to be developmentally appropriate, you might need to share your pain and anger before you are ready to work diplomatically at school.

DON'T CONFRONT...DO CONVERSE!
A direct confrontation is almost never productive when dealing with your team. If the team members go into a defensive mode, it will be very hard to get things done on behalf

of your child. A better approach is to think of your interactions and team meetings as part of an ongoing conversation. The rules of conversation involve taking turns, maintaining a topic and making a genuine attempt to understand the point of view of the other participant(s). Eventually, your team will come to expect this conversational style of working together, and when the team members learn not to expect a potentially upsetting confrontation, they will anticipate more positively the work that you can do together. Even something as simple as beginning with a story about a great activity the teacher did in class or remembering to ask about one of the team member's family events can help create this feeling of friendly teamwork. Sometimes, if you are able, it can be helpful to provide some kind of snack or treat for the group to share together. For one thing, this expresses immediate appreciation for the hard working school personnel, even if you might have to talk about some difficult things in the meeting. For another, eating together creates an automatic environment of social communication, helping you to achieve your ultimate goal of working under conditions of mutual respect and unity of purpose.

My husband Jack was always in charge of IEP snacks. Usually, before the meeting, we strategized about the best type of treats to bring. For an early morning meeting, breakfast foods such as bagels and orange juice seem to help the team "get going." When possible we tried to let the team know in advance what we were bringing to an early meeting so that the hard working staff might be able to save time on breakfast. For afternoon meetings, we found that snack foods that are crunchy and salty – like chips, pretzels or popcorn – can help everyone maintain focus and attention after a long day of work. As a general rule, we have learned that chocolate is appreciated at any hour of the day!

At first, providing these treats was part of a conscious effort to support the members of our team, but eventually we realized that food truly does create a social, friendly atmosphere...somehow it is hard to maintain resentments when you are passing the popcorn! Over the years, our teams came to anticipate that this small pleasure would be a part of the meetings that we had together. At PJ's former elementary school, where he "graduated" so many years ago, the occupational therapist still asks me periodically about Jack and reminisces about all of the special treats that he provided.

While we realize that we are extremely fortunate to have the resources to "cater" our IEP meetings, it has been my experience that any small gesture of appreciation and community spirit will be a positive catalyst for productive team work.

DON'T THREATEN...DO ASSERT!
In this day and age, it is not at all unusual for the specter of lawsuits and litigation to threaten, either implicitly or explicitly, the work done on behalf of complicated children. While even an implied threat might get you something you want in the short term, it is generally not a good strategy for creating an ongoing, positive relationship with the school system in which you are working. This advice does not in any way negate the importance of knowing and exercising your rights as a parent of a student with special needs, which might at times mean involving professional advocates or legal counsel. It is, in fact, extremely important for you to understand the

laws that govern special services in public schools and to have the help you need to gently but consistently assert your rights on behalf of your child. Whenever possible, however, this should be done in the spirit of empathy for the school's often complicated point of view. You may have to make it a point to listen carefully to the school personnel and acknowledge their position before you clearly assert your own.

DON'T BLAME...DO PROBLEM SOLVE!

As discussed previously, the desire to find someone to blame in a difficult situation seems very natural to the human condition. However, as a parent, if you are able to acknowledge immediately that you do not blame the school for your child's problem (remember—even if you strongly disagree with what they are doing, they did not create the original problem), you will be amazed at how quickly they will let go of any blame toward you or your child. It might be hard to make the first move toward letting the blame go, but it will be the only way to look at your child's school difficulties as problems to be solved together. Sometimes a simple statement such as, "Obviously you are not the cause of Sally's problems; we don't think we caused them either, and they certainly are not her fault!" will be enough to get a meeting back on track.

DON'T CRITICIZE...DO SUGGEST!

Educators, especially teachers, are probably among the most under-appreciated and overworked group of professionals in our culture. In this day and age, they are expected to be accountable for many, many things that are out of their control, and if they sense you think that they do not know how to work with your child, they may react in anger and become defensive.

On the other hand, teachers are usually extremely intelligent people who love to learn. If you can present the needs of your special child as something new and interesting to learn about, and if you can provide realistic suggestions about what will help make your child's school world more successful, teachers will be much more likely to be receptive to you and to your ideas. Remember this may take time and some repetition as you help school personnel learn about your unique child.

DON'T ATTACK...DO PERSIST!
Perhaps this point is redundant, and yet, it is a final reminder that you do not have to be combative to be persistent. It is your right and responsibility to advocate for your child and you will be doing this job long after this team of people has moved on to someone else's child. Eventually, your team will come to understand that you are not someone to be feared or avoided, but someone who is going to keep coming back and continue to do whatever it takes to support the success of your child!

By the end of 5ᵗʰ grade, Bob had spent three years in a special education classroom that had gone beyond all expectations in meeting his academic, sensory and emotional needs. We decided to keep Bob at elementary school for one additional year, and to place him in a regular education classroom with a carefully chosen, outstanding teacher. At his IEP meeting it was determined that Bob would be pulled out of the regular class for one hour per day to work on continuing academic and sensory-motor needs in a special education setting.
When school rolled around in the fall, Bob started attending his new general education class. It was quite a transition and while he was optimistic, he reported feeling "invisible" among

all of the kids that he did not know and who did not know him. After about one week, the very diligent special education staff had scheduled his pull-out services. Bob came home upset, saying he was not ready to begin being taken out of his new class. At that point we scheduled a meeting with the team, including Bob, to figure out what to do. In the meeting Bob explained that he thought it would take three more weeks for him to feel like he belonged in his new class and for the other kids to see him as one of them. He also gave feedback about the times of day that he thought would not be okay for a pull-out. I will never forget watching this incredible group of educators sit around the table, seriously considering the point of view of our 11-year-old son, working and re-working the schedule until it felt right to everyone. And as you have probably guessed, he did not begin that schedule of special education services for three more weeks!

The heroes of this wonderful moment are many. Obviously, the extraordinary special education teacher who had spent three years creating, cultivating and nurturing this team on behalf of our son. And, of course, the regular education teacher who not only accepted Bob as a part of her class, but had the ability to make a true space for him within the social environment and believed in the importance of his voice. Then there were the therapists, the evaluation specialist and all the many adults at school who pulled so hard for his success. Finally, there was Bob himself, who somehow found the strength and courage, after having completely failed at school at the age of seven, to try again, to learn to trust the grown-ups and, eventually, to rediscover his own sense of self-worth and success.

When School Teams Don't Work

There are times, however, when no matter how hard we try, we cannot create a positive, productive school team. Critical signals that the team is not a good one for you and your child include when you do not feel that the important members of the team (most especially the teacher) respect your child, are interested in understanding his/her special needs, are able to view accommodations as fair and necessary, and/or believe in your child's right and ability to belong in the educational setting. When, despite your best efforts, the team does not work for your child, the experience can be painful beyond expectation. As a parent who naturally has deep feelings of love and protection for your son or daughter, you will likely feel a great deal of anger toward people that you perceive have been rejecting of or unfair to him/her, and this resentment can last for a very long time. It can be especially challenging if you do not feel that anyone in the larger school community has understood or responded to your concerns. It is critical that you find people who you can safely talk to about what you have experienced, and you should not be surprised if you need to talk about it for a long time after this happens. Sometimes it might also be important to try to take your case to people who have influence in your school system. Perhaps you were not able to change a situation to benefit your own son or daughter, but your willingness to speak up about your experience will possibly help a similar student in the future.

When Bob went into second grade, we had a pretty good idea that his learning disability was substantial and that it was going to be very hard for him to learn the things that were expected of students that school year. However we believed, in spite of his obvious academic deficits, that by following the principles of support, communication and respect, he could have a successful (in terms of self-esteem) and productive (in terms of growth in skills) year. As it turned out, this was not attainable in the class-room in which he found himself. I deeply regret that we were not able to see this soon enough to remove him more quickly from what became a very damaging situation for him. Looking back, I realize that my belief in the team process had become not only a productive way of advocating for my children but also a kind of coping mechanism; my devotion to the idea of promoting and sustaining relationships for the purpose of getting the boys what they needed blinded me to the reality that my son was in an unacceptable situation that no amount of sustained personal effort or skillful conversation would remedy. Through this expe-rience I came to understand both that learning to say "no" could be just as important as relationship building, and that it can be very difficult as parents to balance these two responsibilities as we traverse the school system from year to year...

When you find no alternative other than to leave a school team, you might have a hard time trusting that another group of professionals will be able to do a better job for your child. Some parents have found that home-schooling is a good temporary alternative while they attempt to get their bearings within the school system. For others, providing education at home over the long term becomes the best solution for meeting the sensory, educational and social-emotional needs of their child. Whatever your choices, it is important to have at least a small group of experts to help you traverse the process of raising and educating your child with sensory integration challenges.

...For our family, looking for a new school program for Bob involved researching what was available and meeting teachers and observing in classrooms. As can sometimes happen, the information about alternative programs was not readily available to us – from the perspective of the school system, it was preferable to have students stay in their neighborhood school program. Eventually, though, we were lucky enough to find an incredible match for Bob's needs at a different public school. Little by little, we grew to trust the teacher and the team that would, over the following four years, lead him back to a place where he could learn and receive so much more.

Using Sensory Strategies At Home

If your son or daughter has received an occupational therapy evaluation at a clinic or at school and is receiving services, your therapist may have begun to talk with you about additional strategies and activities that can or should be done at home. The therapist may have recommended a specific book or sent activities/exercise sheets with examples of recommendations. From the perspective of the therapist, this is part of a thorough treatment plan that is developed step by step with family members, specific to the child's needs, so that it can be completed quickly and easily and incorporated into daily routines. However, if you are anything like many other families, you may not be sure about how to fit these recommendations into your life! No matter how thoughtfully prepared by a caring therapist, it might feel overwhelming to you as a parent who wants so much to do everything possible to support your child but at the same time might stress over the responsibility of what one child called, "the dreaded home program."

The truth is, intervention once or twice per week may not be enough at this stage to allow a child establish the sensory foundation to support the development of necessary skills. Even ten minutes each day of supportive body activities can really make a difference in terms of the child's development of quality of movement and consistency of skills. Many families have found that working this activity in before school and/or before homework time can help children be more ready for focused activity. You will likely find yourself needing to try out several different schedules or routines, notice what is working or not working at any given time, and work with your occupational therapist to fine-tune your home program so that it feels manageable, reinforcing and supportive for all of you. Specific ideas to consider for home are provided in *Appendix VI*.

During the elementary school years, most often one or both of our boys were participating in home programs suggested by conscientious therapists. For years, "body games" before school, pre-homework movement activities, and daily eye exercises were a standard part of our world. Sometimes this felt pretty overwhelming, and I learned to put a limit on what I agreed to do – I realized that I either needed to be clear about what was realistic and what we could (or would) actually do at home, or I would have to face up to admitting that we didn't follow through or, worse, pretend that we did when we really did not.

At times, I wondered if I would be following my boys around, facilitating home programs into their adult years. But as they grew into teenagers, they began to learn to understand their own bodies well enough to seek out supportive physical activity (like running, swimming, pull-ups or bike riding) when they needed them on their own. Not unlike, you could say, their parents who met at the pre-dawn aerobics class all those years ago!

Some Resources That Might Help
(Additional Resources in *Appendix I*)

BOOKS
- *Answers to Questions Teachers Ask about Sensory Integration* by Carol Stock Kranowitz
- *Executive Skills in Children and Adolescents: A Practical Guide to Assessment and Intervention* by Peg Dawson and Richard Guare
- *Learning Outside The Lines* by Jonathan Mooney and David Cole
- *Lost at School: Why our Kids with Behavioral Challenges are Falling Through the Cracks and How we Can Help Them* by Ross W. Greene
- *Making it Easy: Sensorimotor Activities at Home and School* by Mary Haldy and Laurel Haack
- *MultiPlay: Sensory Activities for School Readiness* by Gerri A. Duran

- *Playground Politics: Understanding the Emotional Life of the School-Age Child* by Stanley Greenspan
- *Sensory Motor Handbook: A Guide for Implementing and Modifying Activities in the Classroom* by Julie Bissell, Jean Fisher, Carol Owens, and Patricia Polcyn
- *Smart Moves: Why Learning is Not All In Your Head* by Carla Hannaford
- *Social Thinking* by Michelle Garcia Winner (multiple books and therapy materials to support social development available at www.socialthinking.com)
- *The Alert Program® for Self-Regulation* by Mary Sue Williams and Sherry Shellenberger (multiple books, resources and therapy materials available at www.alertprogram.com)
- *Too Loud, Too Bright, Too Fast, Too Tight: What To Do if You are Sensory Defensive in an Overstimulating World* by Sharon Heller
- *Tools for Teachers Plus Other Useful Tools for Parents, Teachers, Teenagers, and Others* by Diana Henry

DVDS
- *"How Difficult Can This Be?" – The F.A.T. (Frustration, Anxiety, Tension) City Workshop* and other DVDs by Rick Lavoie (available at www.ricklavoie.com)
- *"Learning About Learning Disabilities"* by Judith E. Reisman
- *"What the Silenced Say: An Evening with Jonathan Mooney"* available at www.peakparent.org

AUDIO

- *Teachers Ask About Sensory Integration* by Carol Stock Kranowitz and Stacey Szklut

COMMUNITY

- Horseback riding
- Individual Sports (running, kayaking, wrestling, weight training, hiking or swimming)
- Martial Arts
- Music Lessons (such as drumming, singing or blowing an instrument)
- Rock Climbing
- Skiing
- Swimming
- Yoga

6

Middle and High School:
The Road to Transition

As your child gets ready to make the transition from the elementary school setting to middle and then high school, you probably will be feeling the same trepidation as many of the parents around you. In addition, you may be wondering how the specific needs of your child with Sensory Processing Disorder will be met in a new setting where your child might be frequently changing classes and teachers, and where every teacher is dealing with many more students each day. During these transitions it is extremely important to include your child, if at all possible, as an active member of his/her educational team. Growing young people need to have a voice in the type of program that will work for them, and they need practice in a safe environment to learn to advocate for themselves, because they will be required to do this more and more as they move toward adulthood. Is your child aware of the types of sensory support that is needed in order to be as successful as possible in the classroom setting? Does he/she understand the academic modifications that support participation in the regular education curriculum? Does he/she know the words to describe these needs and if so, is he/she able to express them in a way that can be understood and interpreted as respectful by peers and adults in his/her life? These are the types of skills that your child will need to be developing in the coming years.

You probably will find that the emphasis of your child's program begins to change at these times of transition. Sometimes, as children get older, more time and attention is placed on modifications to the environment and compensatory strategies than on interventions for developing specific skills (for example, use of keyboarding or dictating assignments vs. working on fine motor/visual motor skills for handwriting). You will need to decide as a team if this shift in program priorities is appropriate for your child. Either way, it seems clear that the concepts of modification and compensatory support are critically important to children who learn differently as they move through the school years. One of your biggest jobs at this juncture will be to first understand, then be able to communicate to others, that specific adjustments to general education expectations are appropriate, reasonable and in no way diminish your child's successes at school. For example, if your child needs more time to show what he/she knows on a test, this does not provide an unfair advantage. Children who do not have the same special needs would probably benefit very little, if at all, from being given extra time. Because they are able to demonstrate what they know (and consequently what they do not know) in the allotted time, extra time would not likely improve their performance. Similarly, if your child needs a quiet environment to take a test, frequent movement breaks during structured activities, assistance with note taking, audiobooks, visual instructions, opportunities to respond orally instead of in writing, use of a spell-checker or calculator or any of a myriad of other types of support, you must help the child and the school staff to understand that these are merely tools that allow access to learning and participation for this student. Try to think of these modifications as analogous to eye glasses or a wheel chair—when we can remember these concrete examples it is easier to realize that "fair" is not the same as "equal!"

PJ, as a ninth grader, loved biology but had experienced some initial struggles in his high school class with organizing his note-book, getting worksheets done legibly and following specific written directions accurately. For the first time in all his school years, I did not go to school to "interpret" PJ for his teachers – with the help of one special education teacher, he was out there doing it on his own. One day, PJ came home and told me that they were involved in cutting out paper strands to represent DNA during the class period. While my mother brain was already creating a not so pretty picture of PJ with a pair of scissors and long strands of paper in his hands, he went on to say that his teacher had come over and sat down next to him and quietly asked, "PJ, do you have hand-eye coordination problems?" He answered that yes, he did, and she proceeded to take the scissors out of his hand and finish cutting his paper, all the while carrying on a conversation with him related to the content of the biology class. This scenario took place in a public high school with more than 30 students in the classroom. I only met this teacher once during open house night at school, and she will probably never know what hearing this story meant to me - because of her perceptiveness, her sensitivity and her obvious understanding that not every student can show what he knows in the same exact way. After all of the many many school years, this teacher understood something very important about my son without any help from me!

Disorganized Brains Living In an Organized World

One of the most challenging aspects of the transition to middle and high school is the expectation that students will be able to get organized around their daily schedule and school-related responsibilities. For some students, being handed an agenda and given a schedule and school assignments somehow translates into the ability to pull it all together and get down to the business of being successful in their new school environment. For others, however, that agenda becomes just one more thing to lose track of in the bottomless pit of their backpacks!

One of the biggest mistakes we can make with any child is to assume that he/she can learn any particular skill without direct instruction. Just as some children need more direct and explicit instruction to learn reading, math or social skills, some children (not infrequently the same ones who required some other type of direct instruction) need to be taught in measured small steps how to organize their world at school. Some middle and high school programs have "Study Skills" classes that might help with these types of issues, but often, help with organization falls to the grown-ups at home. This can make the topic of homework, not to mention long-term assignments or science fair projects, a sore subject for some tired families! You might find that your older child needs continual support to look at all the components of his/her school work and figure out how to manage it from day to day. This might involve using a calendar for planning ahead, breaking down long range tasks into smaller more manageable units, making specific plans for where things will be kept at various points throughout the school day, searching for needed resources together, learning to contact other students to get information that was missed in school and/or developing strategies for after school time management. He/she might also need reminders about what types of sensory input (e.g., taking frequent movement breaks, eating specific types of snack food and/or setting up the work environment – quiet vs. noisy or light vs. dark - to match his/her sensory needs) will help the work at home be the least stressful and the most successful. This is all not to mention that, for some students with specific learning disabilities, you also might be spending time literally helping them complete the required work!

Again, your child is likely to need specific instruction about how to use school related tools. You might have to start by modeling or showing him/her how to approach the day's tasks – for example, planning a long-term project together using the calendar to map out a plan, organizing a binder in a way that makes sense to him or her, or even developing a check-list to refer to when getting ready in the morning. In addition, some adolescents might need help balancing the requirements of getting their school work done with having the down time they might need even more than their peers. The important thing to remember is that organization will not be achieved by simply purchasing required school supplies or writing down assignments in a planner. Some middle or high school students may be ready to make this leap independently, but adolescents with difficulties processing information from their senses often have not developed all the small competencies that lead to autonomy in the later school years. It also can be beneficial to recognize that some young people will not be very motivated toward achieving organization at this time in their lives. While this may be typical of any child at this age, it is often the case that children with Sensory Processing Disorder develop the motivation and capacity to deal with planning and follow through later than their peers. Patience and a sense of humor are always useful for keeping things in perspective!

Sometimes parents of middle and high school aged students are also surprised to find that their pre-teen or teenaged child has very little concept of the meaning of time. Comprehending time, in fact, is very much tied to our understanding of how our bodies move through time and space. Perhaps your child learned to read a clock when he/she was in second or third grade, but never really understood what it all meant. Or, maybe, like many other children, they never really mastered the clock back then and have been getting by with reading the numbers on digital clocks and watches (digital tools are great but we need to remember that they do not depict, and therefore do not provide any information about, the actual passing of time.) Whatever the case, you may find that now is the age when your child is more receptive to learning concepts of time, although teachers and therapists working with children in this age range might not think to consider the comprehension of time concepts as a goal. This may be a good point at which to check with your team about helping to assess your child's understanding of these critical concepts (e.g., telling time, understanding how the time on the clock relates to the events of the day and knowing how much time it takes to go places or get things done) and possibly developing an intervention plan.

At home it can be helpful to talk about time in specific ways. For example: making guesses about how long it might take to get a thing done and then checking how long the task actually took; talking about what time the clock says and how that matches to what events are happening at that time for him/herself or for other family members, what the daylight looks like, what happened before and what might be happening next. It can also be very effective to use timers that are more visual such as a sand timer/hourglass, egg timer or "Time Timer" (See equipment/supplies in Appendix I) that show the passage of time, and can help your child see the amount of time he/she has, how much time was used and how much time there is left. There are also mobile and desktop apps that some students find helpful. As parents and teachers start to realize that some students actually have very little concept about the passage of time, they can better understand the student's seeming inability to get anything done on schedule. They can also start to appreciate that what can look like a lack of motivation on the part of the student might actually be a response to feeling deeply overwhelmed.

I remember going through sixth grade for the second time with Bob after just having finished it a few years earlier with PJ (or third time if you count when I did my own sixth grade year all those years ago!) Because Bob attended the same small charter middle school that PJ went to, the classes and curriculum were pretty familiar. So on the one hand, the work was easier because I already knew how to do it. On the other hand, it left me sometimes wondering why I had to do the same homework and projects over again when I had already done them just three years before!

When PJ was in these middle school years, I suffered a lot of angst about whether I was helping him too much. How, I asked myself, would he ever develop independence if I sat with him daily during his homework, helped him plan and organize all of his projects and allowed him to dictate his written work to me each night? And what would happen when the work simply became too hard for me? So I worried a lot, but I kept doing what I was doing, because I could not see any other way for PJ to feel successful in middle school, learn everything he needed to learn and still have time to be a young person who desperately needed time in his own, unstructured world.

Yet as PJ approached high school, though he certainly still needed more help than many high school freshmen, the growth in his ability to work independently was extraordinary. He began to do the majority of his work on his own and learned to deal with the consequences of disorganization or lack of planning. He was able to use a word processor for almost all of his written work, though he still dictated to me occasionally when an assignment was overwhelming. He dealt directly with his teachers (though not always as soon as I would or in the way that I would) about problems he was having or modifications he needed to the general education curriculum. And through all this I came to understand that all of the work we did together in the middle school years was, rather than being a roadblock to this independence, the very thing that was needed to help him get where he was able to go. Flashback to crawling, walking, dressing, social interaction, lunch box packing, shoe tying – all of the things that took more time than they seemed they "should" have, that seemed to require so much direct instruction and practice. They just were not going to happen until they did!

So although I sometimes felt irritated by doing sixth grade again with Bob, I was so much calmer and happier the second time around. Because even when the work still took longer than I wished it would, and even if I still wasn't all that interested in World History, I was not afraid. I fully believed that helping Bob was going to give him the best possible chance of being as successful and independent as he would be able to be in his future, and that our work together was simply about moving him forward based on the timeline of his own brain and heart. Taking the fear out of our teamwork together made it, surprisingly enough, at times a lot of fun!

Closing

Life at our house has changed a lot over the years, though some things remain the same. While our boys certainly have not grown out of their sensory processing difficulties, they have "grown into" them in many exciting ways. In addition to periods of direct therapy, they have developed in their ability to use ongoing sensory strategies, self-advocacy and appropriate modifications at school. These have allowed them to work toward their own desired quality of life at home, in school and in their social worlds. As for their mother, I haven't exactly been the fastest learner, but with <u>plenty</u> of practice, I have come to understand, little by little, that each of my sons – just like everybody else – has his gifts and his challenges. My job is actually quite simple: to help them get where they want to go whenever and however possible.

And to do this simple but not so simple job, I am extraordinarily aware of all of the tremendous support I have received from family, friends and Carla along with a whole variety of professionals who have walked beside us every step of the way. Yet I also am indebted to all of the remarkable pioneers in the field of sensory integration who paved the way to our current knowledge of sensory processing and all of its crucial implications, as well as the brilliant and passionate professionals today who continue to provide groundbreaking, creative contributions to the understanding of children such as mine. It is my sincere hope that I have been able to pass on a small bit of their wisdom, along with the "smarts" taught patiently to me by PJ and Bob from day to day. I feel fortunate indeed for all that I have learned and experienced.

Final Words by PJ Wilder

Reflecting on my childhood while reading my own story as a 22-year-old has been an experience that is somewhat difficult to fully describe. It is, of course, a story that is intimately familiar to me. At the same time, I do not remember many of the details of these experiences due to my young age at the time, and the descriptions were not always what I expected to see.

Some things certainly never change— even a brief inventory of my college career would check plenty of boxes describing potential signs of sensory issues in elementary school. I would like to think I have grown into these issues successfully and mastered many of my challenges despite this. For example, having successfully navigated all the parks of the greater Albuquerque metro area as a child, I have moved on to trying to find the novelty I still seem to crave by extending my explorations to the broader world. I have had the opportunity to travel and have lived outside of the country three times in the last four years, including my current residence in Tunis, Tunisia where I am attempting to master the Arabic language.

However, this continuity was not what struck me most while reading through this work. Rather it was the sharp contrasts, reading perhaps in more clear language than I ever had heard before about my childhood struggles with the basics of managing routines, fine motor skills, and information processing that was more than a little jarring to me. As someone who more than once has deliberately taken an unfamiliar route when driving home at night, this was one part of the account that was less expected for me.

For the fact that I have been able to, in many ways, overcome what was such a defining limit of my early life, I am incredibly grateful to my parents and the many teachers, professionals, and friends who worked with me all these years. I have come to realize that the educators who work with young children have an unjustly thankless lot in life. The work they do could hardly be more important and yet they are barely remembered by those to whom they have given the greatest help. Without having read my own story, I would never have truly realized just where I have come from and how lucky I have been.

I wish to offer my sincere thanks to my parents for the countless ways they have worked so tirelessly to give me the opportunities I have had today, and of course to Carla Williams and everyone involved in my early years, as well as the many incredible teachers whose paths I have crossed. I hope that my story has made a helpful contribution to this work and most of all that it can help to illuminate some small piece of the challenges facing educators and parents entrusted with the care of all of our futures.

Appendix I

Additional Resources for All Ages

PRINTED RESOURCES

- *Creating Your Personal Vision: A Mind-Body Guide For Better Eyesight* by Samuel Berne
- *Disconnected Kids: Groundbreaking Brain Balance Program for Children with Autism, ADHS, Dyslexia, and Other Neurological Disorders* by Robert Melillo
- *Emotional Intelligence: Why It Can Matter More Than IQ* by Daniel Goleman
- *Just Take A Bite: Easy, Effective Answers to Food Aversions and Eating Challenges* by Lori Ernsperger, and Tania Stegen-Hanson
- *Keeping Ahead In School: A Student's Book about Learning Abilities and Learning Disorders* by Melvin D. Levine
- *Living Sensationally: Understanding Your Senses* by Winnie Dunn
- *Parenting a Child with Sensory Processing Disorder* by Christopher Auer, Susan Blumberg, and Lucy Jane Miller

- *Raising a Sensory Smart Child: The Definitive Handbook for Helping Your Child with Sensory Integration Issues* by Lindsey Biel and Nancy Peske
- *Sensational Kids: Hope and Help for Children With Sensory Processing Disorder* by Lucy Jane Miller
- *Sensory Secrets: How to Jump-Start Learning in Children* by Catherine Chemin Schneider
- *Special Diets for Special Kids* by Lisa Lewis
- *The Mislabeled Child: How Understanding Your Child's Unique Learning Style Can Open the Door to Success* by Brock Eide and Fernette Eide
- *The Explosive Child: A New Approach for Understanding and Parenting Easily Frustrated, Chronically Inflexible Children* by Ross W. Greene
- *The Out Of Sync Child: Recognizing and Coping with Sensory Integration Dysfunction* by Carol Stock Kranowitz and Jane Miller
- *The Out Of Sync Child Has Fun: Activities for Kids With Sensory Integration Dysfunction* by Carol Kranowitz
- *Sensory Motor Handbook: A guide for Implementing and Modifying Activities in the Classroom* by Julie Bissell, Jean Fisher, Carol Owens, and Patricia Polcyn
  S.I. Focus Magazine (available at www.sifocus.com)

DVD

- *When Our Senses Don't Make Sense: Understanding Sensory Processing Disorder* by Jane Koomar, available at *www.thespiralfoundation.org*

WEBSITES
- Raising a Sensory Smart Child
  www.sensorysmarts.com

On-going information about meeting the needs of children with sensory processing issues, includes courses available, resources, books for children, factual information about sensory processing disorders, monthly tips, and specific activity suggestions.

- OTA The Koomar Center
  www.otathekoomarcenter.com
  OTA The Koomar Center, founded by Dr. Jane Koomar, PhD, OTR, is one of the largest occupational therapy centers in the country, specializing in pediatrics and sensory integration, assessment and intervention.

- Spiral Foundation
  www.thespiralfoundation.org
  Spiral Foundation, a nonprofit organization housed at OTA The Koomar Center, provides continued research and education on sensory integration dysfunction and Sensory Processing Disorder. The site provides information on sensory integration, trainings and resources as well as a newsletter for families and professionals. They also provide a Parent SPD Education toolkit of resources and materials for parents.

- Star Center
  www.starcenter.us
  The Star Center, with founder and executive director Dr. Lucy Jane Miller, provides research-based treatment for Sensory Processing Disorder and other sensory challenges including SOS (Sequential-Oral-Sensory) Feeding Solutions under the direction of Dr. Kay Toomey.

Site provides information about Sensory Processing Disorder, services and news and resources.

- Henry Occupational Therapy Services, Inc.
  www.ateachabout.com
  Diana Henry offers school based and individual occupational therapy services. Site provides information about services, workshops and products.

- Irlen Syndrome/Scotopic Sensitivity
  www.irlen.com
  The Irlen method, developed by Helen Irlen, uses colored overlays and filters in the treatment of perceptually based reading and learning difficulties. Site provides information about "Irlen syndrome", treatment, research, training and workshops, conferences, sample visual distortions and a newsletter.

- Kelly Dorfman, M.S., L.N.D.
  www.kellydorfman.com
  Kelly Dorfman is the co-founder of Developmental Delay Resources and provides services as a health program planner and nutritionist. Site provides contact information, related articles, and a calendar of events.

- Developmental Delay Resources (DDR)
  www.devdelay.org
  Information and resources related to children with developmental delays in sensory, motor, language, social and emotional areas. Site includes provider

directory, related news and events, a newsletter and recommended books and events.

- The Out-Of-Sync Child
  www.out-of-sync-child.com
  Introduces the work of Carol Stock Kranowitz, including available products and events as well as additional resources about Sensory Processing Disorder

- Sensory Processing Disorder Foundation
  www.spdfoundation.net
  Promotes awareness and recognition of Sensory Processing Disorders. Site provides information about membership, treatment, resources, related news, and a newsletter.

- Child Development Media (CDM)
  www.childdevelopmentmedia.com
  CDM provides access to commercially available videos books and curricula on child development and related topics and conducts continuing education, hosts teleconferences and publishes a newsletter

- Brain Gym International
  www.braingym.org
  Provides information about Brain Gym including philosophy, events, and courses.

- Handwriting Without Tears
  www.hwtears.com

Describes a dynamic curriculum for directly teaching handwriting skills to support legible, fluent and automatic handwriting for young elementary school-aged children.

- Dr. Sam Berne, O.D., FCOVD, FCSO
  www.newattention.net
  Provides information about Sam Berne's behavioral optometry practice as well as his many publications and products, upcoming events and other available resources

EQUIPMENT/SUPPLIES
- Achievement Products
  (800) 373-4699
  www.achievement-products.com

- Integrations
  (888) 388-3224
  www.integrationscatalog.com

- Pocket Full of Therapy
  (800) PFOT-124
  www.pfot.com

- School Specialty/Special Needs (Abilitations)
  (800) 444-5700
  www.schoolspecialty.com

- Southpaw Enterprises
  (800) 228-1698
  www.southpawenterprises.com

- Therapro Inc.
  (508) 872-9494
  (800) 268-6624
  www.therapro.com

- Time Timers from *www.timetimer.com*

Appendix II

Some Other Terms You Might Hear

This appendix provides some terms other than those we've discussed in this book. These are terms you may come across in other publications on Sensory Processing Disorder or that you may hear someone use in your IEP meetings.

Adaptive Response: A successful and appropriate response made by a person to an environmental demand.

Arousal: The state of the child's nervous system in relationship to how ready they are to do a given task at a given time. Arousal might be too high, which would look like over activity or difficulty focusing and attending, or too low, which might look like a lack of interest or motivation, whining or low energy. A functional arousal state is one in which the nervous system readiness matches the requirement of the activity.

Attention Deficit Disorder (ADD): A neurological condition characterized by consistent inattention and impulsivity that impacts success in school, in social interactions or in behavior. When there is a pattern of constant, fidgety movement (hyperactivity) the condition is called Attention Deficit Disorder/Hyperactivity (ADHD). At times the child might be distracted by everything around him or her, and at other times might be driven to engage in preferred activities for long periods of time (i.e. television, movies, or video games).

Audiology: The study of hearing, especially hearing deficits and their treatment.

Auditory Processing: the ability to take in and make sense of information that is heard; concerns the ability to process the information rapidly and efficiently enough to comprehend and respond appropriately to spoken language.

Bilateral Integration: The neurological process of integrating sensations from both sides of the body. This is the foundation for bilateral coordination, which is the ability to use both sides of the body together in a coordinated way. This means both arms, both legs, both ears, both eyes and the two sides of the brain. In addition to the right and left sides working together, it also refers to the top and bottom of the body working together as well as front and back. The ability to cross the midline of our body is also a result of good bilateral integration. All of this information from our body helps us understand space and time, the three dimensions, and foreground and background.

Body Scheme/Body Awareness: The mental picture of one's own body. These terms refer to the understanding about where one's body is in space, how one is moving and how body parts relate to each other.

Dysgraphia: A learning disability resulting from difficulty expressing thoughts in writing. Can include difficulties with handwriting, spelling or the rules of written language.

Dyslexia: A language and learning disability marked by impairment of the ability to recognize, comprehend and produce written words. It mostly affects reading and spelling skills.

Dyspraxia: *see Praxis*

Gravitational Insecurity: A vestibular processing problem that often appears as anxiety, distress, panic, or as an irrational or abnormal fear of movement. Children with gravitational insecurity might not enjoy participating in playground activities, might avoid moving surfaces like escalators or elevators, might resist having their feet off the ground or might avoid positions where their head is out of a vertical or upright position (such as lying down, putting their head back or being upside down).

Impulsivity: describes a child's frequent action upon sudden wishes or urges rather than thinking things through.

Kinesthesia: The conscious awareness of body position or movement of the muscles, tendons and joints that allows us to do things with our body without looking.

Learning Disability: Identified difficulties with one or more aspects of academic tasks such as reading, writing or math that are not due to problems with seeing, hearing or intelligence. Alternative educational approaches are often needed to tailor successful learning experiences by utilizing the child's strengths and learning style.

Modulation: The brain's ability to regulate its own activity by determining the importance of the sensory input and then responding appropriately to that input. In a modulated state, the brain is able to take in more information when needed, "shut off" information when it is too much, and "get used to" information that occurs frequently and consistently. When the nervous system is modulated, individuals are able to stay in their comfort zone as they move through the challenges of daily life.

Motor Planning: *see Praxis*

Occupational Therapy: An occupational therapist is trained in the biological, physical, medical and behavioral sciences, including neurology, anatomy, development, kinesiology, orthopedics, psychiatry and psychology. An occupational therapist uses purposeful and fun activities to help a person make adaptive responses that then help the nervous system develop and work more efficiently. When referring to children, this therapy supports their "occupations" which are playing, being a student, being social, using their bodies in a coordinated way, managing their emotions, and participating in daily living activities.

Oral-Motor: Often used to refer to the skills that allow for organized movements in the area of the mouth that affect eating, speech, motor planning of mouth/lip/tongue movements, and self-regulation.

Praxis: The ability to have an idea, sequence the parts, and carry out the plan in a coordinated and automatic way, even if the task is new and unfamiliar, then be able to evaluate the outcome, either during or afterwards, notice if something needs to be changed, then re-execute and evaluate again. Motor planning is often used as a synonym for "praxis" but motor planning is only one part of praxis. "Dyspraxia" is a term used to describe difficulty in the process. Often children with dyspraxia have to think harder and use more cognitive strategies to accomplish movement tasks. They may perform a skill easily one day and be unable to do it on another day. Things like ball skills, shoe tying and meal time skills may be difficult for these children to learn as well as to perfect.

Proprioception: Often called the "position sense," it is the unconscious awareness of information coming into our bodies from our joints, muscles, tendons and ligaments. It helps us to understand where our body parts are and how they are moving in relation to ourselves as well as to the world around us.

Physical Therapy: Improves a child's physical abilities through therapeutic activities that address strength, muscular control and coordination.

Self-regulation: The ability to self-assess how one is feeling (i.e., noticing one's own activity level or state of arousal, or how one is emotionally or physically responding in a situation) and effectively choose an appropriate action or strategy to bring one's nervous system to a state that matches the demands of the situation, activity or task.

Sensory Defensiveness: A tendency to react negatively or emotionally to sensory input that is not typically considered uncomfortable or dangerous. These reactions are often "self-protective" or distress responses that appear to happen more quickly, be more intense and/or last for a longer time than they would for other children in the same situation. These reactions are often called flight, fright or fight responses.

Sensory Diet: A planned and scheduled daily "menu" of sensory motor based activities developed together by a family and their occupational therapist. These activities are strategically planned throughout the day to help the child deal with stress, calm and organize the nervous system, and learn to become more self-regulated. This term was coined by Patricia Wilbarger, occupational therapist.

Speech-language Therapy: Therapy to develop or improve skills in speech articulation, verbal or nonverbal communication, social language skills, oral-motor skills for speaking, chewing and swallowing, voice production and fluency.

Transition: A term used to describe change from one activity, situation or environment to another.

Visual-Motor: Refers to the ability to coordinate information received through the eyes with the head, neck, hands and body in order to perform skilled movements.

Visual-Perception: The ability to take in information from what is seen and make sense of it in order to respond appropriately for the situation.

APPENDIX III

Sample Letters for Important People

At times, the job of explaining your unique little person to other people can become overwhelming. Yet it is important, in so many situations, for you to be able to advocate for your child and help ensure the greatest possibility for success. It is our hope that the following sample "letters", whether used literally as documents to give to someone else or just as some ideas to guide your conversation, will help you in this ongoing work.

Dear _____,

My daughter, Mary, will be a new [patient/student/client] of yours beginning _____. So that you will be able to work with her more easily from the start, I want to let you know that Mary has difficulty with sensory processing.

Sensory processing is the ability to deal with incoming sensory input in an organized way. When this is hard for children, they might be excessively fearful, inexplicably aggressive or they may dramatically avoid certain sensations or experiences. It can be helpful to be aware of difficulties that might be especially challenging in your setting.

FOR THE DENTIST/DENTAL HYGENIST

- Unusual tastes can be hard for Mary to cope with, so she likes to bring her own toothpaste for cleanings.
- Light or unexpected touch can be frightening. Tell Mary, using simple language, what you are going to do and then show her before you begin.
- Deep or firm touch can help. Mary might need to be held tightly by a family member while you are working or she might like to wear the heavy x-ray vest during the entire procedure.
- Lying back in the chair can be very disorienting. It might help Mary to sit up in the chair.
- The sound of the power cleaner or drill can terrify Mary. Whenever possible, please avoid using power equipment. When it is necessary, please warn her before you start. Using headphones to block out the sound might also help.
- Since the whole appointment can be overwhelming for Mary, it can help her to have a distraction like a favorite toy to hold or to listen to a family member tell a story or read a book while you are working.

FOR THE DOCTOR AND OTHER MEDICAL STAFF
- Light or unexpected touch can be frightening, including looking in her ears or mouth or using the stethoscope. Using firm touch during these procedures can help.
- Use simple language. It helps to tell Mary what you are going to do and then show her before you begin.
- Lying back on the examining table can be very disorienting for Mary. It might help a lot if she can sit on a chair during the examination or sit on a family member's lap.
- The visit might become overwhelming for Mary. As much as possible, it can help to take breaks and check in with her to see how she is doing.
- Sometimes it helps Mary to hold a favorite toy that she brings from home.

FOR TEACHERS OR CHILD CARE PROVIDERS
- Light or unexpected touch can be frightening for Mary. It helps if you can give only firm touch and also to be aware of situations where children are very close to each other. These might include circle time (she might need to sit a little apart from the other children or be in a chair), walking in line (she might do better at the end of the line) or getting ready to go home at the end of the day (she might feel safer getting her papers from her cubby after everyone else is done).
- It is hard for Mary to sit still and pay attention. She might move around a lot on the floor or in her seat, lie down on the floor or on her desk or stand up to do class

work. When you can allow her to move around without creating problems for the rest of the class, she will usually be better able to learn.

- Unfamiliar tastes and textures can be hard for Mary to understand. It is okay if she doesn't try all of the snacks that you provide.

FOR INSTRUCTORS OR COACHES

- It can be hard for Mary to learn new things with her body. Patience and understanding, as well as extra opportunities for learning and practice, can help this be a positive experience.
- Light or unexpected touch can be frightening for Mary. Avoiding light touch all together and using a firm touch when guiding her through movements or skills will help her feel safe and learn as easily as she can.
- Simple explanations are easier for Mary to understand. When it is possible to show her something, in addition to telling her in a simple way, it is easier for her to make sense of what you want her to do.

FOR HAIR SYTLISTS

- Chairs that move or spin might be scary for Mary. If she can sit on the floor, in a stable chair or in the lap of a family member, it will probably be easier for her.
- If you usually give treats like a lollipop after the haircut, it can help Mary to get it before she starts because sucking on something keeps her calm.
- Hair washing is really hard for Mary, even at home. Skipping this will make the hair cut easier. Similarly,

the noise of a blow dryer is also hard so we can skip this step too!

- Light or unexpected touch can be frightening for Mary. Using a firm touch can help. It also would be helpful to keep hair off Mary's skin as much as possible and limit the movement of the hair on her head.
- It is hard for Mary to understand unfamiliar smells. Sticking with water or very gentle hair products will probably help a lot, or I'll bring her favorite shampoo to her appointment.

APPENDIX IV

Some Responses for Well Meaning (And Not So Well Meaning) Critics

There is probably no parent who has not had to face an unsolicited and unwanted comment about their parenting from an on-looking relative, friend or stranger. But when children have Sensory Processing Disorder, their behaviors can be harder to understand and therefore harder to "tolerate" by unknowing observers. This makes it difficult for the parents, who are often judged in a way that feels exasperating or unfair. In general, these hurtful comments can be met with one or a combination of the following types of responses:

- HUMOR – A friendly joke can sometimes diffuse an uncomfortable situation.
- EMPATHY – Letting people know that you understand how they feel can help them let go of their need to tell you what they think.

- INFORMATION – Providing information about your child's differences, especially to people who have an on-going role in your life, can allow them to understand what you and your child are dealing with and be more sensitive to your special situation.
- BOUNDARIES – Sometimes you just need to let someone know that you are not open to their opinion or suggestion in a given moment.

The following examples might help you to traverse a challenging interaction –

A relative complains about your son's or daughter's limited eating repertoire, implying that you should insist that they eat something "normal" or "more healthy" at designated mealtimes ("Corn chips for breakfast???")

- HUMOR – "Hey, this is the healthiest breakfast he's ever had!"
- EMPATHY – "It seems strange to see a kid eating corn chips for breakfast. It worries me too but we're working on it each day."
- INFORMATION – "Joey has a hard time dealing with different flavors and textures in his mouth – I've learned to be less stressed about it since we are getting help and he's getting better."
- BOUNDARIES – "We're working on expanding his menu, but it is hard for him so it would be helpful if you wouldn't comment on what he eats."

When the family gets together, a relative makes comparisons between the behavior of one sibling and

another ("Why can't you be a good eater/ sleeper/ play-mate like your sister?")
- HUMOR – "Well, Sarah, I guess you got your picky eater genes from me!"
- EMPATHY – "I know you really worry about Sarah, but she is growing in her own way."
- INFORMATION – "Being in new situations with a lot of people makes it hard for Sarah to feel comfortable and do the things she can do at home."
- BOUNDARIES – "Because we understand that Sarah feels things differently, we try not to make comparisons between the girls."

At Thanksgiving dinner, your little one ends up sitting under the table, much to the dismay of his grandfather ("You need to get back in your seat right now!")
- HUMOR – "I'll bet some of us wish we could get under there too!"
- EMPATHY – "You are really disappointed that everyone isn't sitting at the table for this special holiday. Maybe we could find him another place to be alone for a while."
- INFORMATION – "It is so hard for Tommy to be in noisy, crowded places when he doesn't know what to expect. When he is overwhelmed it helps him be in a small dark place."
- BOUNDARY – "Usually we find if he's quiet for a couple of minutes he'll come back on his own when he can."

Close family friends want to hug and kiss your child, pinch her cheeks, or play with your child's hair causing her to

"melt down" every time they visit ("Look how big you've gotten – come here and give me a hug!")

- HUMOR – "If you think this is bad, you should see how she reacts to people she <u>doesn't love</u>!
- EMPATHY – "I know how you feel, she's so dear I just want to hug her all the time but it upsets her a lot."
- INFORMATION – "Being touched like that is so hard for kids who feel things the way Susie does, but she really likes to shake hands and show you her stuffed animals."
- BOUNDARIES – "Since it feels painful to Susie to be hugged and kissed, we just ask people not to do it. I hope you understand."

Your child has a screaming fit in the grocery store because you are standing on the "wrong" line. Another shopper is giving you an unpleasant look or unwanted advice ("If that were my child, I would teach him how to behave.")

- HUMOR – "I haven't done this since before he was born so I know he didn't learn it from me!" <u>OR</u> "If I were his mother I'd be really upset about this!"
- EMPATHY – "Yeah, this is so loud and embarrassing to see."
- INFORMATION – (It is not really necessary to provide information to strangers. In general it is best to remind yourself that this is your child's behavior and does not reflect on your skills as a parent.)
- BOUNDARIES – "I know you're trying to help but there's something going on here that you don't know about and we are doing okay."

A friend often compares your parenting to her own ("What I did with Maxwell was …)
- HUMOR – "Hey, we'll send her over to you and you can call us when you get her fixed up!"
- EMPATHY – "You're feeling concerned and confused about how Lily acts, but when kids have problems like she does there are special ways of dealing with it."
- INFORMATION – "Lily is different than Maxwell. When children have difficulty understanding information from their touch system…"
- BOUNDARIES – "We're getting professional help and we talk to our therapist about this every week." OR "We're working on a new approach and I am excited that it is going to make a difference."

Your mother-in-law often suggests that you practice the skills that are lacking for your child ("You should try reading/writing/cutting/playing catch with him at home.")
- HUMOR – "Read with him, hey, I knew I forgot something!"
- EMPATHY – "It scares us too when he can't do the things that other children can do, but we understand that he just isn't ready yet."
- INFORMATION – "We are learning that when children have trouble understanding their world with their bodies, it is hard for them to learn different skills. Later, when he gets better with his body we can work on _____."
- BOUNDARIES – "The therapist has recommended that we don't talk about reading yet."

Your best friend expresses frustration about all the control your daughter seems to have when playing at her house ("Why does she have to have everything _her_ way?")

- HUMOR – "Well, she doesn't _have_ to if you don't mind waiting a really long time for the game to start!"
- EMPATHY – "I know, it is very frustrating to have to be so careful with Julia since it is taking her a long time to learn to share. For now we just have to 'pick our battles' carefully."
- INFORMATION – "With sensory integration issues it is very hard for children when things change. Julia feels more secure when she can play the game the same way every time but we are working on helping her be more flexible."
- BOUNDARIES – "We're getting help so Julia can be easier about things like this but for right now it would work better to let her do this her way."

**Many thanks to Suzanne Carlson for sharing her personal experiences and to Debra Sugar for wisdom, insight and humor!

Appendix V

Sensory Support for Infants

- Notice if your baby is giving you consistent cues about preferences for routines around big daily events such as feeding, changing and sleeping

- Make difficult transitions (such as getting into the car or waking from a nap) right before or after feeding time or provide a pacifier during or after activities your baby does not seem to like

- Provide extra-long swaddle time after bathing or diaper changes

- Provide a cotton hat (to add some pressure to the head)

- Try a variety of positions while holding the baby, or while playing or moving around with him/her; for example hold the baby in an upright position, or lay the baby down on his/her back or tummy while bouncing, rocking or gliding.

- Sleeping on a crib sized water bed mattress provides gentle movement through the night - today's crib sized water bed mattresses are designed under government safety regulations and are comprised of a foam encased mattress with water inside

- Commercially available infant swings

- Frequent periods of "baby exercise" where arms and legs are moved and wiggled (could be done with music if the baby seems to enjoy this input)

- Provide opportunities for supervised, playful "tummy time" (i.e. laying on the tummy while looking at something of interest or interacting with a favorite adult)

- Try a variety of sounds such as: different types of music, singing and various voice pitches

- Provide white noise for calming, e.g., fan, humidifier, fish tank, white noise machine

- Notice if your baby calms best with an overall decrease in noise and/or people talking

- Keep your baby out of florescent lights

- Notice your baby's reaction to dark vs. light rooms or changing light stimulation (e.g., moving while facing a window or looking at sparkling lights

Appendix VI

Specific Activities to Try at Home

©2003 OTA the Koomar Center. These activities are reproduced with permission from the OTA The Koomar Center Home Accommodation Checklist by Porder, A., Trecker, A., May-Benson, T., Koomar, J., & Szklut, S. Additional Activities and accommodation checklists for other age groups and settings are available from the Spiral Foundation at www.thespiral-foundation.org.

SENSORY DIET ACTIVITIES:
- To provide deep pressure, try firm hugs, snuggling, gentle pressure to the top of the head, shoulders or feet, and slow massage. Follow your child's lead and let her responses tell you what works best.
- During the day, deep pressure can be provided by wearing a backpack, hat, fanny pack, or by placing heavy objects in his pockets. Wearing a hat can also cut down on extraneous visual input.

- Try pretending to be a burrito and wrap your child in a blanket or a piece of lycra spandex to provide touch pressure to most of the body.
- For general calming at the end of the day, cuddle your child and slowly rock together in a rocking chair.
- Help your child engage in organizing "heavy work" activities that exercise the muscles. Try jumping rhythmically on a mattress on the floor or mini-trampoline, hanging from monkey bars, riding a bike or other riding toy, carrying books and crawling games. Swimming and horseback riding are also great "heavy work" activities.
- If your child likes roughhouse play and deep pressure, try "sandwich squeezes" with heavy pillows. Encourage your child to lift, push, and carry the pillows while you intermittently put her between pillow "sandwiches." With all rough house play, follow your child's lead, allowing her to be in control and giving her time to respond to you and to initiate her own interactions.
- Play "couch" games such as jumping on pillows on the floor, cuddling under pillows, building forts, and climbing on and off the couch.
- An older child may benefit from a supervised exercise program, which could include weight lifting, running or use of aerobic exercise equipment such as a Stairmaster, exercise bike or treadmill.
- For the child that enjoys playing with stuffed animals try exchanging the inside stuffing with heavier material, such as a double secure bag of aquarium gravel, beans or other non-toxic material for increased "heavy work" input.

- If your child seeks a great deal of movement, try providing movement experiences throughout the day. It may help to wake your child 15 minutes earlier before school and allow him to jump on the bed or to swing.
- Eating crunchy or chewy foods such as bagels, carrots, pretzels, lavasch crackers, dried fruit, chewing gum, or fruit rolls can provide organizing oral input. Sucking water through sports bottles or crazy straws, blowing whistles, kazoos, party blowers, and making "raspberries" also provide good input to the mouth.

ENVIRONMENTAL ACCOMMODATIONS:
- Cut down the sensory inputs in the environment by using low lighting, soft rhythmical music or quiet spaces. If your child is overwhelmed, talking to her too much can be disorganizing. Regulate your speech into short, only necessary phrases.
- Keep visual and auditory distractions to a minimum. It may be helpful to have a quiet space in your home with a reduced number of toys. A small tent, a table covered with a blanket, or a large empty box works well as a quiet "fort." A carpet can decrease noise and a beanbag chair or pillows can provide comforting deep pressure.
- Give your child the option of time-out or "quiet time" alone when he feels over-stimulated.
- A quiet area with few visual distractions is also helpful during homework.
- Be aware that bright lights or the flicker and hum of florescent lighting may be disturbing. Use lamps and other lighting alternatives such as full spectrum light bulbs.

Children who are highly sensitive to light may prefer to wear sunglasses.

- Prepare your child for sudden noises. Vacuum and use other noisy appliances while she is out.
- Unexpected touch can be difficult for children who are sensory defensive. Approach your child from the front and provide a warning before touching.
- If your child is over-sensitive to smells, use unscented detergent and shampoo. Do not wear perfume or use car or stick-up air-fresheners. Use unscented markers.
- If your child is over-sensitive to movement or fearful of leaving the ground (gravitational insecurity), provide alternative playground activities. For example, your child may be able to walk across a line on the floor but not able to walk on a balance beam. Limit the amount of rolling or twirling – let your child's response be your guide or check with the occupational therapist.

STRATEGIES FOR RUNNING ERRANDS, PUBLIC OUTINGS, FAMILY GATHERINGS, OR SPECIAL HOLIDAYS:

- Be watchful during stimulating group activities such as birthday parties, family gatherings, recess or lunchtime at school, trips to mall or playgrounds. Your child may be bothered by the large amounts of multiple sensory inputs inherent in these situations. Allow your child to sit or stand on the outskirts of the group and move in as he feels comfortable. It may be helpful to initially spend a short time in these settings, increasing the time as your child's comfort level increases.

- When you know the day will include activities that involve a great deal of sensory stimulation ((e.g., trip to the mall, meals with large groups, family events), structure the rest of the day with calm and organizing inputs.
- Shorten family gatherings or outings as needed. It may be necessary to avoid these all together and have a sitter come stay with your child while you go grocery shopping or to the mall. Sensitive children will generally accommodate better to shopping during less busy times.
- Before entering a potentially stimulating situation, help your child to engage in gross motor movement, such as running or jumping in a safe place, or engage her in "heavy work" activities, such as pushing on the car and pretending to move it.
- If rough housing gets out of control, direct the children to more appropriate gross motor activities such as jumping, marching, or dancing.
- At birthday parties, keep the number of children small and have the party in a familiar, comfortable environment.
- Educate friends and family about the negative impact of unexpected touch and loud voices ahead of time. Advocate for your child if an adult is not respecting his space or discomfort with touch or movement.

STRATEGIES FOR CAR RIDES:
- Having something to suck or chew may help your child remain more organized during car rides.

- If your child is sensitive to touch it may be helpful to cover the car seat with padding such as foam, flannel, or lamb's wool.
- Placing window shades on the side windows can cut down overwhelming visual input and bothersome sun light during the drive. Some children find sunglasses helpful.
- Play calming music during the drive or sing with your child to help him remain calm.
- If the noise of the car is bothersome to your child try having her wear earphones or a headband.
- Provide a place for the child to solidly rest his/her feet or move the passenger seat back so the child can push his/her feet on the back of the seat.
- Calming pressure can be provided through the use of a weighted pad or beanbag on the lap.
- Avoid using strong air fresheners in your car, as many children can be sensitive to this smell.

SLEEP AND WAKE ROUTINES:
- A quiet tape of "easy listening" music, ocean sounds or white noise may be helpful. Some parents report that their children fall asleep more easily when a humidifier, fan or fish tank is turned on and making a soft background noise.
- If your child has trouble falling asleep, try using soft flannel or cotton tee shirt sheets. A heavy comforter or sleeping bag can provide deep calming pressure, which some children like. Children may benefit from having stuffed animals to hug, or sleeping on lamb's wool.

- Putting pillows or large stuffed animals on the edges of the bed can provide a smaller, more enclosed space for sleep.
- Provide window darkening shades and/or curtains.
- Respect the child's choices in sleepwear. Children with tactile sensitivities often prefer soft cotton pajamas without feet. Some children prefer tighter fitting pajamas that provide touch pressure; others prefer lightweight, loose clothes.
- Do very active games one hour before bedtime for about 20 minutes (e.g., dancing, jumping, or swinging).
- Some children need to be awakened with calming stimuli such as a back or foot rub, oral input, or gentle rocking. Limit the conversation for this child.
- Some children require intense input to wake up. Try jumping up and down on the bed with hands held, cold face wash, electric toothbrush, lively music, and strong flavors at breakfast (e.g., orange juice made with less water, lemonade or tangy jelly).

EATING, BATHING, SELF-CARE AND DRESSING:
- If your child is over-sensitive to food in her mouth, try giving ice pops or frozen juice ice cubes to desensitize the mouth. Carefully applied firm pressure around the mouth prior to eating might also be helpful.
- For children who have difficulty brushing their teeth, a Gerber Nuk brush or a toothbrush with natural bristles can be more acceptable. Some children might prefer a vibrating toothbrush.

- If haircuts are a problem, give pressure to the head or shoulders; for nail cutting, give pressure to the hands or fingers. At times visually distracting your child with a book or video during these activities can be helpful. If your child is extremely sensitive you may find that performing these activities when she is asleep works best.
- For children who dislike baths make sure to warm the bathroom prior to undressing. Using a smaller tub can make your child feel more comfortable. Encourage water play to make the experience fun.
- To help with showers, try a hand held showerhead to control the spray and keep water out of the yes. Pouring rinse water from a small pitcher or using a visor or dry wash cloth to cover the eyes may be helpful. Count to "10" while pouring water so he knows it will end. When washing hair allow your child to sit upright as tipping the head backwards may be frightening.
- If your child is overly sensitive to smells use unscented shampoo and soaps.
- When getting out of the bathtub, use a large towel to wrap the child tightly. Have your child reach out one arm or leg at a time and rub it firmly with another towel to decrease tactile sensitivity.
- Some children prefer either tight or loose fitting clothes. Be aware of your child's preferences in clothes and buy accordingly. All cotton clothes often work well. Wash clothes several times before your child wears them.

References

Ayres, A.J. (1973). *Sensory integration and learning disorders.* Los Angeles, CA: Western Psychological Services.

Ayres, A.J. (1979). *Sensory integration and the child.* Los Angeles, CA: Western Psychological Services.

Ayres, A.J. (2005). *Sensory integration and the child 25*th *anniversary edition.* Los Angeles, CA: Western Psychological Services.

Cohn, D.J., & Donnellan, M. (1998). Including the family perspective in sensory integration outcomes research. *American Journal of Occupational Therapy, 52.*

DeSantis, A.M. (2001). *The Relationship Between Early Colic, Excessive Crying, and Sensory Processing at 3-8 Years of Age.* Boston, MA: Boston Univeristy.

Fisher, A. M., Murray, E.A., & Bundy A.C. (1991). *Sensory integration theory and practice.* Philadelphia, PA: F.A. Davis.

Greenspan, S., & Greenspan N. (1985). *First feelings.* Dallas, TX: Penguin Books.

Karp, H. (2004). The "fourth trimester." A framework and strategy for understanding and resolving colic. *Contemporary Pediatrics, 21* (2), 94-116.

Laurel, M. (2000). Bringing sensory integration home: A parent perspective on the alert program for self-regulation. *Autism/Asperger's Digest*, March-April.

Laurel, M., & Williams, C.C. (2000-2005). *Sensory integration for learning and development: A practical team approach.* [Workshop presented at multiple locations].

May-Benson TA, Koomar JA and Teasdale A (2009). *Incidence of pre-, peri-, and post-natal birth and developmental problems of children with sensory processing disorder and children with autism spectrum disorder.* Frontiers in Integrative Neuroscience. 3:31. doi: 10.3389/neuro.07.031.2009

Miller, L.J. (2006). *Sensational kids.* New York, NY: Perigee.

Oetter, P., Richter, E.W., & Frick, S.M. (1995). *M.O.R.E. Integrating the mouth with sensory and postural functions.* Hugo, MN: Professional Development Press.

Richter, E.W., & Oetter, P. (1990). Environmental matrices for sensory integrative treatment. S.C. Merrill (Ed.). *Environment: Implications for occupational therapy practice - a sensory integrative perspective.* Rockville, MD: American Occupational Therapy Association, Inc.

Trott, M. C., Laurel, M.K., & Windeck, S.L. (1993). *Senseabilities: Understanding sensory integration.* Tucson, AZ: Therapy Skill Builders.

Wilbarger, P., & Wilbarger, J.L. (1991). *Sensory defensiveness in children aged 2 -12.* Denver, CO: Avanti Educational Programs.

Wilbarger, P. (1995). The Sensory Diet: Activity programs based on sensory processing theory. *Sensory Integration Special Interest Section Newsletter.* Bethesda, MD: American Occupational Therapy Association.

Williams, M.S., & Shellenberger, S. (1996). *"How does your engine run?" A leader's guide to the alert program for self-regulation.* Albuquerque, NM: Therapyworks, Inc.

Winner, M.G. (2000). *Inside out: What makes a person with social cognitive deficits tick?* San Jose, CA: Think Social Publishing Inc.

Winner, M.G. (2004). *Organizing organization.* [Workshop in Albuquerque New Mexico].

About the Authors

Marci Laurel, MA, CCC-SLP, has been a speech-language pathologist for more than thirty years, specializing in sensory processing disorders related to communication. She currently works at the University of New Mexico Center for Development and Disability, where she provides assessment, consultation, and training related to children with autism spectrum disorder and their families.

Carla Williams, OT/L, has been an occupational therapist for nearly thirty years, specializing in treatment of children with sensory processing disorders. She is owner and director of KidPower Therapy Associates, a multidisciplinary therapy clinic serving the Albuquerque area.

Carla and Marci have lectured nationally and internationally on sensory processing challenges and together these colleagues have authored a book on this topic. Their collaborative work, *Our Hearts' Desire*, is a highly practical guide that is also heartfelt and deeply rooted in Marci's personal experiences as a parent, shared with Carla as therapist to her two now grown sons, who struggled with some of the issues described in the book.